APPALACHIAN WITCHCRAFT FOR BEGINNERS

APPALACHIAN
WITCHCRAFT
for Beginners

The History, Remedies, and Spells
of a Rich Folk Magic Tradition

AUBURN LILY

callisto
publishing
an imprint of Sourcebooks

> To all the witches
> who came before me.

Interior and Cover Designer: Linda Snorina

Art Producer: Sue Bischofberger

Editor: Chloe Moffett

Production Editor: Jaime Chan

Production Manager: David Zapanta

This book is not intended as a substitute for medical advice from a qualified physician. The intent of this book is to provide accurate general information in regard to the subject matter covered. If medical advice or other expert help is needed, the services of an appropriate medical professional should be sought.

Published by Callisto Publishing LLC C/O Sourcebooks LLC

P.O. Box 4410, Naperville, Illinois 60567-4410

(630) 961-3900

callistopublishing.com

Printed and bound in China

OGP 2

· CONTENTS ·

· INTRODUCTION ·

Welcome, wandering witch. I am so honored that your magical path has led you here, to these pages. Whether you are a seasoned witch hoping to learn more about Appalachian witchcraft or you are just beginning your journey, I hope this book provides a safe, cozy space for you to learn and to explore your innate gifts that align with the magic of these mountains.

My name is Auburn Lily, and I moved to Asheville, North Carolina, when I was just seventeen years old. I moved here for university and had no idea I was also entering a deep mystery school by putting down roots here. I wasn't necessarily raised on the magical path, but as my understanding of witchcraft expanded, I recognized all the ways magic was laced into my upbringing. Whether I was being taught an enchantment by an unsuspecting grandmother, learning how to make a simmer pot from my mother (who just wanted to make the house smell better), or heeding omens and superstitions, in retrospect, I found magic in every memory.

When I moved to Asheville in 2009, I met a magical group of people. We encouraged one another to follow our intuition and research the magic that inspired us the most. This led us to explore meditation, crystal magic, lucid dreaming, and astral projection—all of which I had experienced by the time I was eighteen years old. My interest piqued, I found myself drawn into the local witchcraft shops, learning about candle and herbal magic from the wise women I met there. Slowly, my magical practice became an important part of my daily life; routine became ritual.

In 2017, I found myself managing a metaphysical shop in downtown Asheville, and suddenly, I was "out of the broom closet," so to speak. I spent my days helping other witches gather altar supplies and craft spells, holding space for them on their journeys. This is when I knew I was being called out of my lifestyle as a solitary practitioner and being initiated as a guide. Since then, I have been offering magical services to my community, even after leaving the shop in 2020. Now magic is my entire life. It feeds me, literally and spiritually.

After a childhood of moving up and down the East Coast, my journey into Appalachian witchcraft felt like a homecoming. These mountains have revealed themselves as my friends, my familiars, and my ancestors. Through my practice with Appalachian folk magic, I have become empowered to cocreate my reality alongside the forces that be, to take greater responsibility for my emotional and physical health, and to trust my intuition as sacred intelligence. I hope that through this book, I'm able to hold space for you to make the same discovery that I did: there is magic flowing through your veins, and Appalachia is calling.

· HOW TO USE THIS BOOK ·

This book is part reference guide, part spell book. In part 1, you will be introduced to the original Appalachian witches—where they came from, how they lived, and the magic they worked. You will begin to build a solid foundation with them as your magical ancestors, learning all the ways we still incorporate their beliefs and practices into modern-day witchcraft.

Part 2 is a book of spells, guiding you through tried-and-true rituals, meditations, and spellwork. These practices range from brief, 10-minute meditations to hour-long rituals. The spells contained in this book are literally pages from my own personal grimoire (spell journal), and as you work the magic contained here, I recommend that you start your own. As you read on, you'll find instructions for keeping your own grimoire to help you as you grow your practice and continue on this magical journey.

The first time you read this book, I recommend that you read it cover to cover. Because Appalachian witchcraft was inspired by the beliefs and traditions of so many cultures from all over the globe, I find that it's critical to honor those diverse foundations before working any of the spells contained here. But after your first reading, I hope this book can serve as a useful ally to you on your journey as you flip to the chapters that serve you best in the moment. Whether you turn to the spells here to re-create them exactly or you use them for inspiration as you create your own, I hope that through these pages we develop a magical kinship and walk this path together, side by side.

PART I

INTRODUCTION TO APPALACHIAN WITCHCRAFT

The first part of this book serves as an introduction to the ways and wisdom of Appalachian witchcraft. In these pages, you will meet the original Appalachian witches and learn about their beliefs, practices, and traditions, which stem from cultures all over the world. You will learn about how they practiced magic, where they drew their power from, and how the natural world shaped their craft.

You will also be guided in bridging connections to the land and the spirit realm in a way that honors the original practitioners of Appalachian folk magic. Throughout this section, you will build a solid foundational understanding of what Appalachian witchcraft was, what it has evolved into today, and how you fit into this practice as an Appalachian witch.

As part 1 progresses, it shifts from teaching you about the old ways to helping you shape your own practice and journey. You will learn about the power of certain magical tools and how they influence your spellwork, including herbs and natural ingredients. By the end of part 1, you will be ready to begin dabbling in Appalachian folk magic, guided by the spells in part 2!

CHAPTER 1

The Origins of Appalachian Witchcraft

The tradition of Appalachian folk magic has diverse roots. "Folk" means people, so "folk magic" quite literally means the magic of the people. Learning about the rich history of this practice and its original practitioners is an essential part of beginning your journey with Appalachian witchcraft.

In this folk magic lineage, tradition is passed down generation by generation, evolving a bit each time. This chapter takes you on a journey from the origins of Appalachian folk magic through present day, paying respect to all those who paved the way for us to practice magic today. You will learn about both the influence of different cultures and religions on the practice and the kinds of magic the original "granny witches" practiced in their communities.

Understanding the origins of Appalachian folk magic will guide you on your own path as you begin to establish a connection to the earth, your ancestors, and the magic within you. By the end of this chapter, you should have a clear understanding of the roots of Appalachian folk magic, providing a strong foundation for your own practice as an Appalachian witch.

What Is Appalachian Witchcraft?

Appalachian witchcraft is an eclectic folk magic practice that blends traditions from many different backgrounds. European settlers brought their wisdom and practices from Scotland, Ireland, and England, and once they arrived in Appalachia, they adapted their traditions to include Indigenous American, African, and German teachings.

The result is a folk magic tradition that incorporates a multifaceted approach to witchcraft, infused with intuition and wisdom from all over the world, grounded and localized by a deep relationship with the land in Appalachia. Sometimes called "granny magic," these traditions date back to the eighteenth century and include practices like divination, herbal remedies, protection spells, midwifery, and more.

Often, Appalachian folk magic practitioners were the only known healers in their communities, as this rural region did not have many doctors or options for professional medical care. Instead, granny witches were sought after during times of strife and sickness—known for their ability to combine faith and magic to heal, manifest, and foresee. People turned to them for many things, including healing wounds, curing sickness, increasing fertility, and assisting births, as well as protecting the home and working with the land for an abundant harvest.

In essence, Appalachian witchcraft is a way of practicing magic, or directing universal energy, that's influenced by the wisdom of those who walked this land before us. This type of magic is inherently focused on living in right relationship with the land, elements, plants, animals, faith, and unseen energies to generate healing, protection, and good fortune for the community.

How Appalachian Witchcraft Differs from Other Forms of Magic

In the modern witchcraft landscape, there are so many different "paths" or labels for the type of magic that is practiced. Some identify as green witches, crystal witches, or kitchen witches—and the list goes on. Appalachian folk magic is an eclectic path that blends many practices together, and it cannot be contained by just one of these labels. In your folk magic practice, you could incorporate crystals like the crystal witches, work with plants like the green witches, and create magically imbued remedies like the kitchen witches, all in one day—even in one spell!

I believe that the only thing Appalachian folk magic truly requires is a deep reverence for the land and the traditions of Appalachia. There is not a rigid set of rules for practicing this type of magic, whereas some other magical traditions require some kind of initiation, belief system, or specific methodology. In this way, the Appalachian folk magic practice is different from other forms of magic because it is a melting pot, harmoniously blending magical paths together in a way that is unique for each practitioner.

In a modern practice, the known traditions and your intuition are the two main guidance systems for your magic. As you continue to read this book, pay attention to what inspires you and what lights you up. This is where the magic lies for you. Investigate and explore these areas and gather wisdom about them, and soon you'll develop an Appalachian folk magic practice that is uniquely yours.

The Origins of Appalachian Folk Magic

European settlers arrived in Appalachia in the eighteenth century, mainly from Scotland, Ireland, and England. The settlers brought the experience and wisdom of their European roots with them, but they were not well-versed in the intricacies of the Appalachian landscape. Much of the herbal and land-based wisdom that is rife in Appalachian folk magic is credited to the wise guidance of Indigenous Americans in the region, namely the Cherokee and the Yuchi people, though the Iroquois, Shawnee, and Powhatan people are also native to the Appalachian Mountains.

Eventually, German settlers began to work their way southward and influence the tradition as well. Then, in the late eighteenth and nineteenth centuries, the practices were heavily impacted by the African traditions of formerly enslaved people. So, as you can clearly see, although Appalachian witchcraft was mainly practiced by European settlers and their descendants, it was crafted and shaped by the experiences and wisdom of many cultures, and this is an important aspect to keep in mind and honor throughout your practice.

A powerful way to stay in touch with the origins of this tradition and ensure the integrity of your own practice is to make yourself aware of the history of the traditions you incorporate into your practice. Until the American Indian Religious Freedom Act of 1996, the U.S. government restricted Indigenous peoples' access to their own practices, many of which had been shared with European settlers. Appalachian folk magic incorporates quite a bit of Indigenous wisdom, so some of the ways that we can stay in right relationship with the origins of our practice are to support Indigenous land sovereignty movements and to learn about the original keepers of this land. Check the Resources section (page 144) for information on learning about the Indigenous history of the land where you live.

Today, Appalachian witchcraft is a way to work with the natural world and traditions of the region to reach a certain goal, whether it is healing, manifesting abundance, protecting your home, or attracting good luck. Your practice will be influenced not just by these original practitioners but by everyone who came after. As you develop your practice, staying in right relationship with the origins of these traditions and keepers of the ancestral wisdom will only enhance your workings.

How Early Appalachian Folk Magic Was Used

Although many granny witches were solitary practitioners, meaning they primarily worked alone, many of their workings were for the benefit of their communities. As you've already learned, Appalachian folk magic practitioners were often the only healers in their areas, so within the practice there was an innate focus on curing disease, mending wounds, tending pregnancy and birth, and so on. They were a critical part of their communities, bringing not only healing on a physical level but also a sense of spiritual rejuvenation.

However, Appalachian witches were not strictly practicing healing arts. They often practiced divination, protection magic, and dream work, as well as what we now call manifestation magic—using spells or charms to generate a specific outcome. They crafted herbal teas to prevent unwanted pregnancies, wards to protect the home, and much more. This required a wealth of knowledge surrounding the use of herbs, stones, and other natural influences (like the weather or the elements) to generate the desired result.

The primary focus of Appalachian folk magic was—and is—improving day-to-day life, whether by soothing physical pain, bringing about good fortune, or invoking any number of desirable circumstances. Appalachian folk magic practitioners also used magic on a personal level, improving their own lives as well as their communities', and in a modern practice, one of the ways we can pay homage to the origins of these traditions is to consider the greater good in all workings.

Folk Magic Stems from the Natural World

Fostering a deep connection to nature is perhaps the most important piece of the Appalachian folk magic tradition. There is so much to be learned by studying the world around you. The trees tell us when it is going to rain by flipping their leaves upside down. The stripe on the back of a woolly worm speaks to the intensity of the coming winter (a thicker stripe means a more severe season). In Appalachian folk magic, nearly everything in nature has a deeper meaning, and the ability to interpret these messages from nature was crucial to the Appalachian way of life. If we look back to the origins of this practice, we can see that the livelihoods of many Appalachian people depended on being fluent in the language of the land.

Not only can we turn to nature to predict the future, but working intimately with the earth allows us to know where, when, and what to harvest for our spellwork. When incorporating wildcrafted (or foraged) herbs, it is important to know the physical and magical properties of the plant, how abundant that herb is in the surrounding area, and the safe and sustainable way to harvest it. This is both a practical and an intuitive practice—minding what we know to be true while also opening ourselves to lessons directly from the earth and the plants.

Appalachian witches weave together meaning and magic from many different natural sources, like the mountains themselves, the stars, and more.

The Mountains

The Appalachian Mountains are one of the oldest ranges in the world, having formed between 1.1 billion and 541 million years ago. These crystalline mountains extend through a large part of the eastern region of the United States, stretching up into Canada and even continuing in western Europe as the Caledonian mountains. The Appalachian folk magic tradition beholds these mountains as wisdom keepers, as sources of a deep and resonant power, and as a protective fortress. The mountains provide a stable and grounded energy for all workings, and often, offerings are left to the mountains as if they are ancestors themselves.

The Four Seasons

The four seasons set the stage for what type of magic may be practiced at a given time. Working within the rhythm of the year is a powerful way to enhance your practice. In spring, it is common to practice fertility magic and plant seeds, literally and metaphorically. When the sun is at its most powerful in the summer, the energy is harnessed to bring new manifestations to light. Autumn is a time for harvest magic and preparing for the dark night of winter. Then, in winter, the focus turns to nourishing kitchen magic and releasing what no longer serves.

The Sun, Moon, and Stars

The incorporation of astrology—the study of the movements of the sun, moon, and stars and their relative positions as experienced from earth—into Appalachian witchcraft allowed harvests and magical workings to be aligned to the celestial rhythm.

Harvests were decided by the phases of the moon. Appalachian witches believed the waxing and full moon phases were the time to harvest crops that grow aboveground because the energy in the plant was being pulled toward the moon. When the moon was waning or new, they harvested crops that grow belowground, as the energy was receding into the roots.

The Elements

The five elements are earth, air, fire, water, and spirit. Earth is the body, the plants, the mountains, and the soil. It is called upon for grounding and foundational support. Air is the breath, the wind, and the smoke, used for cleansing and clarity. Fire is the flame, the digestive system, the inner spark, and the heat. It is called upon for inspiration and manifestation. Water is the rain, the streams, the lakes, and the waters of the womb, used for cleansing and activating wisdom. Finally, spirit is the unseen and the ancestors, called upon for guidance and energetic support.

The Weather

Predicting the weather was incredibly important for Appalachian witches. Living off the land requires understanding weather patterns in a way that is sometimes taken for granted in the modern age. Too much rain could ruin a harvest. Crops planted too early could be destroyed by a late frost. A heavy snow could endanger the livestock. Appalachian witches had many ways of working in rhythm with and predicting the weather. The sun and moon were often used to predict weather patterns. For example, as the old saying goes, "A ring around the sun or moon, rain or snow is coming soon."

There Is No Wrong Way to Practice Folk Magic

Appalachian witchcraft is an eclectic folk magic craft, with various traditions and beliefs stemming from many different cultures and passed down through many generations of practicing families. Often, what was practiced within a family line had a lot to do with that family's unique heritage. A practicing family with German roots may have been more inclined toward astrological workings than a family with Irish roots, who may have been more focused on faith-based healing.

Spells, charms, and other traditions often vary from family to family and witch to witch. Nowadays, Appalachian folk magic practitioners might not have any family ties to the original roots of the folk magic practice. A lot of modern-day witches only have a magical lineage through study—through books, mentorship, and friendship. There are no hard-and-fast rules surrounding what qualifies as true Appalachian folk magic or a true practitioner!

Folk magic is meant to be informed by the "folk"—the people. This means that as time goes on, folk magic naturally evolves with the practitioners themselves. With scientific advances, increased access to medical facilities, new magical discoveries, and decades' worth of creative spell writing, oftentimes a modern-day practitioner is doing work that looks and feels a lot different from what the original granny witches did. Not only is that totally okay, but it is to be expected! Appalachian folk magic was always meant to evolve alongside the Appalachian witches. There is no wrong way to practice folk magic, because *we are the folk.*

The Influence of Christianity on Appalachian Witchcraft

An important facet to keep in mind when considering the rich history of Appalachian folk magic is that most of these original practitioners, European settlers, were fleeing their home countries due to religious persecution, so their expression of their faith-based belief systems was of high importance. Their religion was of such great significance that, rather than renounce their faith and accept another, they traveled across the seas to the new world. This heavily influenced Appalachian folk magic as a whole.

Many viewed their curative workings as acts of faith-based healing, as holy work. Rather than viewing their practices as being in opposition to religion, many believed they were doing religious work. These original practitioners were not viewing their herbal salves and sachets as magical and witchy creations, but as working with the fruits bestowed upon them by their God. They often referenced the Bible in their spells and incantations, calling directly upon their God in ceremony. In fact, if we could rewind time and ask these granny witches how to describe their practices, most would likely emphasize the power in their faith, rather than call their practice "witchcraft" outright.

These original practitioners were retroactively declared "granny witches," and by all accounts, rightfully so. Clearly, the origins of this practice are rooted both in religious faith and in what is now clearly seen as witchcraft. Although a modern-day practice doesn't require a specific declaration of religion, it is important to note that the Protestant faith is embedded in its origins.

WHAT'S THE RELATIONSHIP BETWEEN RELIGION AND MAGIC?

Generally speaking, there is an incredibly tense—and historically violent—relationship between religion and witchcraft. Typically, this was a one-sided fight. The witch trials that took place all across the globe are perhaps the most tangible evidence of the struggle between these two paths, perpetuated by religion. In multiple verses, the Bible declares outright that witchcraft is a sin, especially in the books Deuteronomy and Leviticus. These verses state that witchcraft, divination, mediumship, spellwork, and sorcery are inherently evil and that these are essentially the workings of Satan himself. Often, the belief was that witches sold their souls to the devil, effectively giving up their place in heaven in exchange for more power on Earth.

The generally held Christian belief was that drawing on any source other than God was inherently witchcraft, so the nature-based power structures in witchcraft did conflict with the beliefs of the church. In this way, the line between religion and magic is drawn based on systems of power. Is God the almighty, or is it nature? Many Appalachian witches drew on the power of God and the Bible, but they also used their nature-based wisdom to influence, to craft, and to heal. Despite this friction between magic and religion, Appalachian folk magic is undeniably rooted in the Christian faith, is influenced by the region's Baptist and Protestant belief systems, and often used the Bible in spellwork.

To this day, many people in the South practice "folk magic" without calling it that outright. Simple charms, superstitions, and spells are passed down as "family traditions" without any conscious relation to witchcraft, even in religious families.

The Bible as a Book of Spells

For many families in the South, the family Bible served as a record of births, deaths, and marriages, and Bibles were often passed down as sacred family heirlooms. For Appalachian folk magic practitioners, the Bible also served as an incredible resource for faith-based spellwork. Most of the time, the verses used in folk magic were intended to protect or heal the subject. Although many verses from the Bible could be used in incantations and spells, the Book of Psalms was, and remains, a favorite.

The Psalms are poetic in nature, as they are sacred songs or hymns, lending themselves to be easily adapted as incantations during spellwork. Each hymn has a different focus and therefore a unique magical association. For example, Psalm 4 begins:

> "Answer me when I call to you,
> O my righteous God.
> Give me relief from my distress;
> be merciful to me and hear my prayer."

This particular psalm was often used for ridding a subject of a bad situation or a streak of bad luck. The psalm continues:

> "I will lie down and sleep in peace,
> for you alone, O Lord,
> make me dwell in safety."

So this same psalm was also invoked for protection and banishing nightmares, often for children.

There are 150 psalms in total, with multiple magical uses for each one, and this is just one book in the Bible! In this way, Appalachian folk magic practitioners were able to use the Bible as a book of spells, incorporating the holy text into their workings more often than not.

The Use of Dolls in Folk Magic

The use of doll babies, or poppets, is a form of sympathetic magic, meaning that the dolls are symbolically linked to a person to have influence over them. This was a common practice in Appalachian folk magic and is still very popular today.

Doll babies can be crafted out of many types of materials, but perhaps the most classic poppet is created out of fabric filled with cotton and herbs that correspond to the intentions of the spell. Once the doll is created, it is linked to the intended subject in some way. Though the most popularized method is sewing in a lock of the person's hair, linking can be done in many ways: embroidering or writing the person's name onto the doll, making it look like them in some way, sewing their photo inside the doll, or simply setting the intention as you create the poppet.

In popular culture, these are often called "voodoo dolls" and have a strong negative connotation, but these dolls can absolutely be used to bring about positive results. I believe the stereotypical view of voodoo dolls is largely due to media portrayal of Vodou, a religious tradition with roots in West Africa. The term "voodoo doll" simply refers to a type of doll crafted in the Louisiana Vodou tradition, while the term "poppet" is broader and applies to traditions across the globe. In my personal practice, I prefer to focus on favorable, rather than baneful, magic because I do not believe in interfering with the free will of others. Poppets are no exception to this rule for me. Doll babies can be crafted to protect someone, to bring them abundance, or to heal them of an ailment. You can even create a poppet to represent yourself to improve your luck, heal your inner child, enhance your self-love, generate prosperity, and more.

The Role of the Modern Appalachian Witch

Today, Appalachian folk magic still exists as an earth-based magical practice, extending far beyond the Appalachian Mountains. The modern-day witch honors many of the original traditions, beliefs, and spells that have been passed down through generations, but there are also substantial differences, as the practice has evolved over time.

THE IMPORTANCE OF APPALACHIAN FOLKLORE

"Folklore" refers to a set of stories passed down through the generations. The folklore of the Appalachian region is an important part of weaving together the past and the present through the power of storytelling. Folklore tends to have a lesson or moral behind the story and typically lends a unique perspective to events of the past. Some folklore is passed down as a way to keep children safe, warning them of monsters that lurk in the woods or deep waters. Some tales attempt to explain the seemingly unexplainable.

The story of the Brown Mountain Lights is a popular Appalachian folktale, and if you were to travel to Morganton, North Carolina, today, you would likely find references to the story around the town. The Brown Mountain Lights refer to eerie orbs of light hovering over a mountain in the Morganton area. The story goes that long ago, many men were lost in a battle between the Cherokee and the Catawba people, and the lights belong to torches carried by women searching for their loved ones.

Another prominent Appalachian folktale centers around the Moon-Eyed People, a race of short, bearded, light-skinned people with giant blue eyes that were ultra-sensitive to sunlight. They were a nocturnal species, at odds with the Cherokee, and eventually, under the light of a full moon, the Cherokee drove them away.

A lot of modern-day practitioners do not affiliate themselves with the Christian faith, although they may still borrow some potent verses from the Bible. Many practicing Appalachian witches began their journey with Appalachian folk magic because they felt ostracized by the prominent faith here in the Bible Belt. This is arguably the reason why many turn to this particular folk magic practice, which actively connects them to both the earth and their ancestors, providing them with a sense of community and kinship.

Appalachian folk magic remains an eclectic path with elements from many different lineages, and it is still imbued with strong Celtic, African, and Indigenous American influences. In many cases, the modern Appalachian witch does not come from a family that openly practices magic, yet incorporates family traditions that have strong, obvious roots in folk magic. For example, I distinctly remember my mother teaching me how to make a simmer pot at a young age, with ingredients that blessed our home not just with a delicious scent but also with abundance and protection. This came to her naturally, but the magical undertones were not her focus at all. Most Appalachian witches I have met over the years share similar stories.

Ways to Practice Appalachian Witchcraft

Because the roots of the practice and its traditions are so diverse, there are truly countless ways to practice folk magic. Each Appalachian witch has a practice that is completely and uniquely their own, influenced and informed by their ancestral lineage, their intuition, their own innate wisdom, and their natural skills and abilities. Some witches lead short and simple ceremonies, while others perform intricate rituals with many tools, aligned with the most potent astrological events. No matter what their practice looks like, each witch embodies Appalachian magic in a way that is powerfully authentic.

As you build your own Appalachian witchcraft practice, you may notice that some methodologies resonate more with you than others. For example, you may be instantly drawn to candle magic but find that you do not have much of an interest in crafting poppets. Trust in yourself and in your intuition to guide you to the traditions that are meant for you.

It would be nearly impossible to cover every single aspect of Appalachian witchcraft, so instead, we will focus on some of the most popular and important methodologies. In part 2 of this book, you will learn spells that correspond with the following themes.

Strengthen Your Connection with the Land

Fostering a deep connection with the earth is one of the most important aspects of developing your folk magic practice. Appalachian witchcraft is innately an earth-based practice. The land itself is an ancestor to us all and one of our greatest teachers. As you build a relationship with the land—both the land you live on and Appalachia itself—you may begin to channel its wisdom, understanding plants, animals, the elements, and life-force energy in a way that you never have before. Being in relationship with the land is also a powerful way to stay grounded as you practice magic.

Heal with the Power of Nature

The earth is absolutely overflowing with allies for magical healing. From herbs and crystals that enhance curative rituals to the elements, which can be utilized for transmutation, nature is a powerful healer. As you continue to grow your connection with the earth, you will learn which natural allies resonate with your intention and empower your magic. In a meditative state, you will be able to call on the elements to enhance your workings. By nurturing a deep relationship with nature, you can transform these tools from inanimate objects or meditative concepts into true allies that weave your magic alongside you.

Cleanse Your Space of Impurities

Every single thing we do and say within a space leaves an energetic imprint. Imagine your home as a chalkboard, and every action taken or word spoken becomes writing on the board. In a very short amount of time, that chalkboard would become a cluttered mess. On an energetic level, this is what happens in our homes on a daily basis. Developing a cleansing ritual is a way to clear out stagnant or negative energy within your home. You will learn a few simple charms and rituals that will help you cleanse your space and wipe the slate clean.

Support Your Personal Relationships

Working magic to nurture your relationships can be a powerful way to strengthen your bond, grow closer, and even transcend difficulties. When rooted in love, these workings often trickle out into other areas of your lives, improving not just your connections to one another, but attracting beauty in many different facets of life. In times when it may be best to let each other go, folk magic can also support you in peacefully cutting ties when you are ready to move on. Soon, you will learn how to impact your relationships in numerous magical ways that serve the highest good.

Conjure Protective Spells and Charms

Setting and enforcing boundaries is one of the most potent ways to step into your power as a witch. When you declare what you will and will not accept in your life and work magic around that declaration, you can access a level of sovereignty that is genuinely unparalleled. You will learn powerful ways to protect your home, your family, your assets, your mindset, your personal power, and even your future—ways that do not interfere with the free will of anyone else. Think of your protective magic as your energetic security system, shielding all that you deem sacred.

Craft Doll Babies and Poppets

In my experience, crafting doll babies, or poppets, is a great way to connect to the roots of this folk magic tradition. This particular practice dates far back into the origins of Appalachian witchcraft, so as you are sewing, stuffing, and enchanting your own dolls in the present, you are moving in rhythm with the granny witches of the past. You will learn how to craft poppets for many different intentions, like attracting good fortune, banishing bad dreams, increasing self-love, and more.

Practice Candle Magic and Fortune Telling

Candle magic and fortune telling are both gateways into the future. Working this type of magic is a surefire way to develop your psychic intuition, open your third eye, and enhance your innate manifesting power. With candle magic, you can influence the future through enchantment and spells, and you can even use the flame and the wax as divination tools. Fortune telling, or divination, refers to peering into the future and receiving insight surrounding what is to come. You will learn different tried-and-true methods to both predict the future and influence it in accordance with your highest path.

Claim Your Roots and Embrace Your Heritage

Connecting with your own ancestral lineage is a way to honor the foundation of the Appalachian folk magic tradition, regardless of whether or not you have roots in Appalachia. You do not have to have a magical lineage to claim your identity as a witch. Remember that the original Appalachian witches were European settlers, carrying their heritage and traditions across the seas and into the lush mountainscape. Appalachian magic is a melting pot of many different cultures, and your unique lineage is a welcome addition. Learning more about your heritage may guide you as you begin to develop your folk magic practice, giving you a sense of what types of magic your ancestors may have practiced if they were Appalachian witches themselves. You may find that you are naturally gifted in traditions that resonate with your ancestry.

Today, there are many ways you can learn more about your lineage, whether or not you have family members to ask or access to a DNA test. Often, learning more about your ancestry can be as simple as researching the last names of your ancestors down the family line. If you are adopted, I recommend looking into the lineages of your ancestors both by birth and by adoption, if you have access. If you are unable to find out your heritage in this way, don't worry. We naturally carry the codes of our ancestors in our DNA. As you continue in your magical journey, the mystery may begin to reveal itself.

Key Takeaways

Appalachian folk magic is a rich and diverse practice that continues to evolve over time. Understanding and honoring the origins of Appalachian witchcraft provides a solid foundation as you begin your own magical journey.

♦ Appalachian witchcraft is an eclectic folk magic craft, with various traditions and beliefs stemming from many different cultures and passed down through many generations of practicing families. Often, what was practiced within a family line had a lot to do with that family's unique heritage.

♦ The primary focus of Appalachian folk magic was and is improving day-to-day life, whether by soothing physical pain, bringing about good fortune, or invoking any number of desirable circumstances.

♦ Fostering a deep connection to nature is perhaps the most important piece of the Appalachian folk magic tradition.

♦ Each Appalachian witch has a practice that is completely and uniquely their own, influenced and informed by their ancestral lineage, their intuition, their own innate wisdom, and their natural skills and abilities.

♦ Connecting with your own ancestral lineage is a way to honor the foundation of the Appalachian folk magic tradition, regardless of whether or not you have roots in Appalachia. You do not have to have a magical lineage to claim your identity as a witch.

CHAPTER 2

Understanding Appalachian Folk Magic

Now that the foundation for your magical practice is established, you can begin to expand your understanding of some of the most influential aspects of Appalachian witchcraft. From interpreting signs and omens to connecting with your ancestors to receiving messages from spirits, unlocking the wisdom of this lineage allows you to build your practice in a way that honors the original Appalachian witches.

In this tradition, belief holds so much power. Throughout this chapter, you will be introduced to some of the most important beliefs in the Appalachian lineage and how they shaped the practice, and you will begin to understand why those beliefs are still upheld today. Whether it's honoring an old superstition or heeding a symbol in a dream, the original beliefs of this practice enrich our modern magical journeys.

This chapter guides you to connect to your ancestral lineage and the spirit realm to strengthen your practice. You will also learn more about the power of your intention and the importance of your dedication as you journey deeper into Appalachian magic. By the end of this chapter, you should be acquainted with many of the beliefs that influenced the original practitioners and still hold deep resonance today.

Acknowledge Your Ancestral Spirits

Connecting with and honoring your ancestors is a potent way to build a solid foundation for your Appalachian witchcraft practice. Even if you don't have ancestral ties to the region, the support of your lineage is a powerful addition to your magic. Remember, the roots of this folk magic tradition spread far and wide, bridging beliefs from all around the globe.

As you build a relationship with your ancestors, you can also make offerings to them that fit their unique or cultural preferences. You can dedicate an altar space to your ancestors and offer food, drink, and beautiful decor. For example, if your ancestors were Irish, you may want to include potatoes and clover in your offerings. You could also include things like your family crest, photographs, religious symbols, family heirlooms, and more. Follow your intuition and make these offerings from your heart!

Establishing a strong connection with your ancestral lineage can increase your psychic ability as your ancestors begin to act as guides who seek to protect you and bring blessings your way. It's important to note that when you are calling on your ancestors, you want to call on "the loving ancestors" or "the well ones." Some of our ancestors are still working out their karma and their trauma, and this can negatively influence your magic. As your practice develops, you can begin to do work to heal your lineage, but when you are first starting, you want to focus on calling in a supportive and uplifting energy.

Utilize the Earth's Energy for Healing and Protection

Working with the earth itself is a vital part of this folk magic practice on a physical and practical level, as well as spiritually and energetically. Physically, the earth provides us with many tools that we can use in our magical workings, like herbs, crystals, soil, and water. On an energetic level, the earth is called upon for grounding, cleansing, protection, and transmutation—shifting energy from negative to positive.

Many spells passed down through the generations call for the use of resources from the earth. Peppermint, abundant in the Appalachian region, has been used for easing cold symptoms as well as for settling the stomach. Witch hazel can be used for dowsing—divining water sources hidden underground—as well as treating skin ailments like scrapes or minor burns, because of its astringent properties. Plants like rosemary, sage varieties, lavender, and more were also burned, as the smoke can be used for energetic cleansing and was often used along with prayer to "take the fire out" of wounds, especially burns. Water can be used for cleansing, charged with a specific intention, or infused with a blend of herbs for a charming cup of tea.

You can also call on the spiritual nature of the earth in your workings. In chapter 4, for example, you will learn a grounding meditation that allows you to clear your mind, cleanse your energy, and empower your workings. The earth is like a living ancestor, here long before us, but still providing its magic in the present day.

The Power of Words from the Bible

Many original Appalachian witchcraft practitioners had strong religious roots, and the settlers in this region were largely Protestant. Incorporating the Bible into folk magic practice came naturally to the Appalachian witches because, for many, the teachings of the Bible were a strong part of their belief system, and there is innate power in belief. When many people believe in something, that archetype gains power. So the Bible was powerful not only because the Appalachian witches held belief in its power but also because the subjects of the witches' curative workings, the members of their community, were often religious as well and believed in the power of the word of God.

Acting as a book of spells, the Bible contains many verses that were used for healing ailments, calling in blessings, and more. For example, Isaiah 58 calls upon God for healing:

"Then your light will break forth like the dawn,
and your healing will quickly appear;
then your righteousness will go before you,
and the glory of the Lord will be your rear guard.

Then you will call, and the Lord will answer;
you will cry for help, and he will say: Here am I."

Working with the Bible as a magical tool often eased tension between religion and witchcraft in Appalachia. Knowing that the working was rooted in faith put the subjects of the spells more at ease. This was how many Appalachian witches evaded scrutiny, despite the Bible declaring outright that witchcraft was a sin.

Significant Signs and Omens in Appalachian Witchcraft

Interpreting signs to predict the future was an important part of the Appalachian folk magic tradition. An omen is a sign or an occurrence that indicates a specific outcome, though the word often carries a negative connotation. Generally, people use the word "sign" to indicate a positive prediction and "omen" when the outcome is negative. Being able to glean meaning from the world around them gave practitioners a sense of peace even if the message was negative, because it made them feel they were able to better prepare for the future.

People in the Appalachian region are still known today for being highly superstitious, and "old wives' tales" are passed down through the generations as warnings to heed while going through life. Even if they did not always come true, omens have worked as cautionary tales, allowing people to prepare should these predictions come to fruition. No harm ever came from canning extra food to prepare for a harsh winter that turned out to be mild!

Countless omens were well-known in Appalachia, each with unique interpretations. Many of them fall into one of two categories: predicting good luck or predicting misfortune. Here are a few examples that are still prevalent today (see page 24).

WHAT IS THE DIFFERENCE BETWEEN A YARB DOCTOR AND A WITCH?

A yarb doctor was a practitioner who only relied on herbal remedies for healing, without any magical or supernatural influence. "Yarb" means "herb," so these herbal doctors were using their knowledge of the medicinal qualities of the plants in the region to cure illnesses. In most cases, neither the witches nor the yarb doctors were educated in traditional medicine, and the roots of their wisdom were similar—combining knowledge from their own ancestry with that of the Indigenous American and African populations in the region.

Especially in strict religious households, yarb doctors were preferred over those who incorporated magic into their practice. Yarb doctors were often thought to be more aligned with the will of God. Where Appalachian witches were calling on energetic and spiritual influences, yarb doctors either exclusively called upon the power of God or took a more "scientific" approach and focused solely on the proper blend and dosage of herbs. Often, there was not a tangible difference between the herbal remedies used by the witches and these yarb doctors—the only difference was the intention and the incorporation of magical influence.

Another difference is that while many original Appalachian witches were women—hence the popular term "granny witches"—yarb doctors were often men. While there were certainly men who practiced magic and women who became yarb doctors, this may be another reason yarb doctors were seen in a better light in their communities. Historically, women were affiliated with the negative aspects of witchcraft, as exemplified by the witch trials.

A Black Cat

Most people know that in some cultures, a black cat crossing your path is considered an omen of bad fortune. It is said that when they cross your path or they are seen walking away from you, they are stealing your good luck and running off with it. It's recommended to turn around and walk quickly in the opposite direction. However, a lesser-known belief is that if a black cat comes into your life and makes itself at home with you, they are blessing your house with prosperity and abundance. Perhaps this is the reason black cats are the classic witch's familiar!

Dreams

Interpreting dreams was, and remains, a popular way to predict the future. Sometimes, dreams offer a literal glimpse into the future; these are called prophetic dreams. Other times, we are left to interpret the symbols within the dreams themselves. For example, dreaming of a lizard could mean a confrontation with a rival. Dreaming of death was believed to predict that someone you knew would be getting married or having a baby. It was also believed that if you dreamed of someone who was deceased and you called their name aloud in your sleep, it was an omen of bad fortune.

An Owl During Daylight

Seeing owls during the day was seen as a negative omen, affiliated with misfortune or even death. Hearing an owl during daylight hours meant that you were about to receive bad news. The hoot of an owl is not to be confused with the call of the mourning dove, however, which is not only common in the morning hours but also represents love coming into your life. Generally, anything appearing "out of time or place" indicated a negative outcome. Another example of this would be plants blooming out of season—this was thought to indicate a harsh winter and scarce harvest.

Tingling Body Parts

A tingling or itching sensation in different parts of the body often held a specific meaning. A tingling or ringing in your ears meant that someone was talking about you. The same feeling on the soles of your feet meant that you would be embarking on a journey soon. An itch on either eye predicted good luck was on its way to you. This sensation in the hands was affiliated with money—itching on the left palm indicated abundance was on its way to you, while on the right, it meant that you would soon have to pay a debt.

THE SIGNIFICANCE OF BIRTHMARKS

Birthmarks were often regarded as signs or omens in the Appalachian folk magic tradition. The general public was divided on the meaning of birthmarks. Some believed birthmarks represented a kiss from an angel, while others believed they were the mark of the devil. Some believed birthmarks were caused by things the mother had done while pregnant, like sinning or eating the wrong food. In truth, the cause of birthmarks is unknown. However, folk magic has an explanation for nearly every type of birthmark you can imagine.

The placement of each birthmark was believed to predict specific qualities or life experiences for the infant. Birthmarks were also thought to indicate the potential strengths and weaknesses of the child as they aged. For example, a birthmark on the legs indicated that the child might struggle to gain independence and stand up for themself, while a birthmark on the feet meant they would travel the world. For a birthmark on the right side of the forehead, it was believed that the child would be highly intelligent, while one on the left side meant they would be irresponsible. A birthmark on either hand predicted great talent and skill.

In a modern practice, it is sometimes believed that birthmarks hold meaning from our past lives. Some say our birthmarks indicate a serious wound we endured in a past life, while others say they are where we were kissed by our soul mate. Beliefs surrounding birthmarks are vast, varied, and significant, even today.

Appalachian Superstitions

Even though traditions and beliefs differ between families, there are many widespread superstitions in Appalachia that are still prevalent today. Superstitions created a set of communal rules that were not meant to be broken, unless you wished to attract bad luck or misfortune. It's hard to know exactly how some of these superstitions began, but it is fair to imagine that they are anecdotal in nature—that once upon a time, someone walked under a ladder and a series of unfortunate events transpired, and word spread.

Even though these superstitions may not have any real impact on our lives and our higher minds know that, many people, myself included, follow some of them without a second thought. For my entire life, every time salt has spilled, whether I've been with friends or family, we've thrown salt over our left shoulder as a reflex. Passed down through the generations, superstitions have become an ingrained part of our lives, especially in Appalachia. Similar to interpreting signs and omens, living by these superstitions gives us some sense of influence or control over our luck. Here are a few superstitions that are still alive and well in Appalachia today.

Always go out the same door you came in.

Especially when visiting a new place or someone else's home, it was believed that it was important to exit the same way you entered. Otherwise, you would be attracting bad luck, both for yourself and your host. I think it's likely that this was a form of practicing "energetic hygiene"—a way to ensure you were not leaving behind any negativity and were instead collecting all of your energy on the way out the door. I do remember hearing this throughout my childhood, and back then, I rationalized it by thinking it was so I could not possibly get lost.

If you spill salt, throw a pinch over your left shoulder.

This is a superstition I still live by to this day. If you spill salt, you are supposed to use your right hand to sprinkle a bit over your left shoulder to avoid bad luck. Also, if someone else spills salt and it falls toward you,

you should both throw it over your shoulder. I am a clumsy person, so I've spilled my fair share of salt throughout my life, and I still toss a pinch over my shoulder every time. Salt is a powerful tool in magic, so I'm not taking any chances with this superstition!

Don't walk under a ladder.

This superstition is likely rooted in practicality and safety; you should never walk under a ladder, especially if it is leaning up against a building. When I heard this as a kid, it made perfect sense to me because walking under a ladder seems pretty dangerous by nature; the ladder could easily fall and injure you. However, the superstition takes it a step further and says that crossing under a ladder is actually bad luck. If you do find yourself walking under one, the superstition says, you should walk backward and find a way around it rather than turning around, to reverse the bad luck.

Always say "bless you" after a sneeze.

It was believed that when we sneezed, our souls could leave our bodies. Outside of hygiene, this was also why it was important to cover the mouth during a sneeze—so that the soul wouldn't escape. It was considered important to "bless" the person who sneezed so that their soul remained intact and in the grace of God. In the South at least, saying "bless you" is simply considered good manners, and it's likely that not everyone who practices this realizes the superstitious roots of the practice. I still say "bless you" after anyone sneezes, even strangers, just in case.

Don't go outside with wet hair.

This was a superstition I heard a lot growing up, especially from my grandma: if you go outside with wet hair, you'll catch a cold, or worse, "catch your death!" Going outside with damp hair, especially in cold weather, was not only thought to make you sick but also believed to attract bad luck. This was an absolute hassle to me as a child, as I never wanted to take the time to dry my hair. Lucky for me, there's no scientific evidence to back this up, so this is a superstition I let slide as an adult.

Communicating with Spirits for Guidance

Similar to connecting to your ancestral lineage, communicating with spirits is a way to access wisdom and insight beyond what is physically available to you as an individual practitioner. Appalachian witches sometimes worked with the spirits of deceased family members or wise elders within their communities for continued guidance from them after their deaths. Spirits can carry messages from other parts of the world, provide perspective on the past and repeating patterns, and even help predict and prepare for events of the future. Spirits, or what some would call "ghosts" or "interdimensional beings," can become part of what I like to call your "spirit team," joining your ancestors to protect you, bless you, and work your magic alongside you.

Depending on the strength of your psychic abilities, messages from spirits can be received in a number of ways. Perhaps the most popularized method is by using a Ouija board, but I do not know many practicing witches who use this as their main form of communication with the spirit realm. Instead, some use pendulums. A pendulum is a tool, often made of a crystal point on a metal chain, used to indicate "yes" and "no" answers based on the direction that the pendulum swings. Others use tarot or oracle cards to interpret the messages, while some people receive messages directly, as if the thought is simply occurring in their mind—this is often indicative of claircognizance, or "clear psychic knowing." You may even begin to receive messages through the appearance of certain animals or a ringing in your ear. No matter how the message is received, the bond can be strengthened by responding to or acknowledging the communication in some way.

Be Careful When Calling upon Spirits

Not every spirit has your best interests at heart, so it is important to call upon them with discretion. Some spirits wish to wreak havoc or cause harm, and that is simply unwelcome in your folk magic practice. Working deeply with the spirit realm is sometimes thought to open a door to more malevolent, demonic energy, so proceeding with caution and practicing regular protection magic is required, at least in my book.

There are many ways to protect yourself, your energy, and your home while you are working with spirits. Some choose to wear charmed jewelry or a cloak meant to protect the wearer. Regardless of what additional methodology you choose, I believe it is crucial to have powerful wards, or protective force fields, in place before working with or invoking spirits at all. Wards act as protective barriers around yourself or your home that do not allow negative energy to enter.

In chapter 8, you will learn how to create a ward for your home, but before you do that, it's important to first clear out any energy that may be lingering in your space. Herbal allies like sage varieties (garden sage tends to thrive in Appalachia), cedar, and rosemary are known for their protective qualities. Burning these herbs in your home with all the doors and windows open can help expel negative energies and entities from your home. Once this has been done, a ward can be put into place to create and enforce strong energetic boundaries.

The Use of Charms in Appalachian Folk Magic

A charm is a talisman or an expression imbued with magical intention. Ranging from simple sayings to herbal sachets, amulets, and bells hanging on a door, charms are an important piece of any Appalachian folk magic practice. Charms can be physical items, or they can be sentences or rhymes that are spoken or sung aloud.

A classic folk magic charm is as simple as placing your broom upside down at the entryway of your home to prevent negative spirits from entering and encourage any unwanted guests to leave. Some of the silly singsong rhymes I remember from childhood actually serve as charming incantations in a folk magic practice, like the classic "Star light, star bright, first star I see tonight, I wish I may, I wish I might, have the wish I wish tonight." There's also the blessing my grandmother taught me to sing each night when I saw the moon for the first time: "I see the moon, and the moon sees me. God bless the moon, and God bless me!"

These days, my standby charm is my lucid dreaming herbal sachet. Hand-sewn and filled with lavender, mugwort, and rosemary, this small bundle gets tucked into my pillow every night before bed. Traditionally, lavender is used for promoting a restful sleep as well as protection from evil spirits. Mugwort is a known ally for lucid dreaming, while rosemary wards off bad dreams and is thought to aid in remembrance—in this case, helping me remember my dreams.

What Are Folk Rites?

Folk rites refer to a set of ritual traditions that are a common practice in the region. While practices vary from household to household, folk rites are more of an established structure for magic that typically centers around the changing of the seasons, phases of life, or special events in the community. Rites can also be focused on healing or religion.

One type of folk rite is a quincunx rite, which utilizes a specific geometric pattern (four items arranged in a square and one item in the center) to quicken the manifestation of spellwork. These items can be positioned in alignment with the cardinal directions to increase effectiveness. For example, in a quincunx working for abundance, you might place herbs or stones that align with your intention—say, peppermint, cinnamon, and green aventurine—at the four directional points and light a candle in the center.

A healing rite that was passed down through my family is what I now know to be a transference rite, which means that a disease is passed from a person into an inanimate object. When I was a child, my knees were absolutely covered in warts. It started with one on my right knee, and by the time I was in middle school, the warts had multiplied. At one point, I had more than a hundred, covering both knees. I tried many methods of removal with no luck. Then one day, my mom said she wanted to try something. She sliced a potato in half, rubbed it over both of my knees, and spoke a prayer over me. Then she buried the potato. As time went on, the warts started to fade away. To this day, I have not had a wart come back. This is a transference rite in action!

Be Clear with Your Magical Intentions

Your intention is your most powerful resource when practicing magic. Especially when you are casting a spell or performing a ritual, keeping your intention at the forefront of your mind is what anchors your magic in reality. Each step of the way, you want your focus to be on what you are intending to manifest.

If you lose sight of your intent, sometimes the spell might skew in a different direction, especially since many of the tools you might incorporate can be used for multiple outcomes. For example, rose can be used to attract a lover and to heal the heart. But if you are grieving, it likely is not the best time to attract a new love. This is why intention is key. If you are performing spellwork and you realize your mind has wandered, simply speak your intention aloud. This is incantation; the power of your voice gives life to your magic.

Certainly, spells and charms call for certain tools, but without a clear intention, your magic will never come to fruition. For this reason, when I am adding herbs, crystals, or other allies to an altar or to a spell, I call on the item by name and by its intention. For example, if I am adding lavender to a spell jar, I will say, "Lavender, for peace," rather than simply stuffing the petals into the jar. This is not totally necessary, but I find it to be a potent way to enchant my creations.

Invite Good Luck into Your Home

The Appalachian folk magic tradition was innately centered around creating your own luck. Many of the superstitions and omens were believed to be linked to fortune, and following suit, much of the magic practiced was either to attract good luck or to banish misfortune. There are many ways to welcome good fortune into your home and your life, from simple charms to intricate rituals.

It was believed that charming a horseshoe and hanging it over your door, pointing upward, was a way to bless the home—a practice that has roots in Romani culture and spread throughout European folk practices.

Appalachian witches also created poppets with similar intentions, imbuing the subject with good luck. There were also Bible verses used in spells for good luck, like Psalm 112:

"His children will be mighty in the land;
the generation of the upright will be blessed.
Wealth and riches are in his house,
and their righteousness endures forever.
Even in darkness light dawns for the upright,
for the gracious and compassionate and righteous man."

One of my favorite spells for good fortune is crafting a cinnamon dish to keep my spare change by the door of my home. To do this, you'll need to create cinnamon dough (1 cup cinnamon, ½ cup applesauce, ½ cup school glue), shape it into a shallow dish, and allow it to harden. If cracks appear, you can use water to smooth them out during the drying process. Once it's dry, you can add your loose change, and you have the perfect ally for manifesting prosperity and luck in your home.

Preparing Your Mind, Body, and Spirit

Before beginning any spellwork, it is important to first calm the mind, body, and spirit. When we practice magic from a centered and harmonious place, our workings are potent, inspiring, and magnetic. I prefer to prepare myself for ritual through a brief, but thorough, meditation. I begin by closing my eyes and deepening my breath. Then, I scan my body for any type of discomfort or tension and find a way to release it, sending the breath there, stretching my limbs, and lengthening my spine. Finally, I will focus all of my power on my intention for the spell or ritual working. Once I feel clear and grounded in that intent, I will open my eyes and begin to craft my magic.

I find this process of stilling and centering the mind before practicing magic to be incredibly important. Otherwise, the magical process could easily become hasty and ultimately irresponsible. For example, if you are aiming to create stronger protective boundaries because someone close to you has hurt you in some way, if you do not first take the time to calm your nervous system and focus your intention on protection, you could be performing magic from a place of chaotic emotion that has negative effects on your reality. What started as protective magic could wind up being baneful (harmful or destructive) magic. While some people do practice this type of magic, it is not something that I recommend, as the ramifications are usually intense and unwanted.

Have Patience with Yourself and Your Practice

Although we each have an incredible intuitive capacity and innate skills, building a magical practice takes time, patience, and dedication. As you begin to create your Appalachian folk magic practice, it is important to be gentle with yourself as you learn. Sometimes, we have the tendency to push ourselves to perfection—to have every herbal remedy memorized, be able to identify every crystal, and see every spell come to fruition. But the truth is that it's called a "practice" for a reason.

Rather than trying to absorb and embody every facet of Appalachian witchcraft from the very beginning, take steps each day to align with your own innate magic. Set aside time each day to dedicate yourself to some aspect of this practice. Maybe one day, you research your heritage to connect more deeply with your ancestors, and the next, you create an altar to your ancestors and meditate. Taking small, sustainable steps is the perfect way to build a practice that lasts and continues to support you throughout your life.

The media and popular culture have created quite an image of witchcraft, with flowing robes, bubbling cauldrons, and intricate spells, but the truth is, the magic is in the journey. I recommend keeping a journal, or a grimoire, to chronicle your magical discoveries. In it, you can take notes on what you learn about your ancestors, create resource pages for future reference (like the different uses of herbs and stones), and write out the step-by-step instructions for your spells so you can re-create them in the future.

Key Takeaways

Appalachian magic is primarily centered around healing and manifesting good fortune. We can honor the foundations of the practice by using our magic to improve the lives of those around us, as well as our own.

◆ Establishing a strong connection with your ancestral lineage can increase your psychic ability as your ancestors begin to act as guides who seek to protect you and bring blessings your way.

◆ Communicating with spirits is a way to access wisdom and insight beyond what is physically available to you as an individual practitioner. Spirits can carry messages from other parts of the world, provide perspective on the past and repeating patterns, and even help predict and prepare for events of the future.

◆ Especially when you are casting a spell or performing a ritual, keeping your intention at the forefront of your mind is what will anchor your magic in reality.

◆ Before beginning any spellwork, it is important to first calm the mind, body, and spirit. When we practice magic from a centered and harmonious place, our workings are potent, inspiring, and magnetic.

◆ Although we each have an incredible intuitive capacity and innate skills, building a magical practice takes time, patience, and dedication.

CHAPTER 3

Preparing Your Tools and Ingredients

N ow that you have deepened your understanding of the Appalachian folk magic tradition, it is time to prepare for working your own magic. Throughout your journey, you will make use of many different tools, natural ingredients, and herbal allies in your spells and rituals. In this chapter, you will learn how to responsibly and sustainably source these natural materials for your craft, and how this can deepen your connection to the earth and to your magic. You will be introduced to some of the most popular tools used in Appalachian witchcraft and guided in their uses. You'll also learn about some of the potent herbal allies and their uses in magical and curative workings.

So far, you have been immersed in the rich history, beliefs, and traditions of Appalachian witchcraft. This chapter serves as a preparation for casting spells and performing rituals, guiding you in building your witchy arsenal of tools, herbs, and other natural resources for your spellwork. By the end of this chapter, you should feel ready to begin practicing your craft! This is the final chapter before you begin part 2, which is a book of spells to get you started on your magical path.

Stay Open to New Experiences and Insights

Although understanding the origins of the practice is important, your journey with Appalachian witchcraft will be uniquely yours. Keeping an open mind and trusting your intuition will be crucial as you embark on this magical path. Part of the fun of practicing magic is exploring new methods and learning what resonates through your own experience. Remember, this tradition is a melting pot of many different magical and spiritual lineages, so there are countless ways to practice Appalachian folk magic. Allow yourself to experiment with different kinds of spells and remedies, especially while you are just beginning your journey as a witch.

As you begin to hone your craft, keep in mind that locally sourcing your ingredients for spells and remedies is preferred, but not required. When it is possible, it's definitely ideal to responsibly wildcraft, or forage, your materials, like herbs, soils, waters, crystals, and more. When you cannot find the ingredients you need in nature, the next best thing is to find a local shop run by the witches in your community. If you live in an area where witchcraft is not as popular, you can also do some research to find a small shop in a neighboring area that you can support by shopping online. Sourcing within the magical community, rather than ordering from faceless retailers, is a great way to ground your magic in a network of reciprocal support, even when you are a solitary practitioner. It's also a good way to befriend fellow witches!

Begin by Cleansing Yourself and Your Space

Before beginning any magical working, it is crucial to start with a cleansing ritual. You can purify the space, yourself, and your tools through many different methods, like burning herbs, using an intentional mist or spray, or practicing meditation and prayer. Sometimes, you may also want to use a mix of a few different methodologies depending on what spell or ceremony you are crafting. For example, if you are doing a self-love spell, you might start by burning rosemary for cleansing and protection and then spray the altar space, yourself, and your tools with rose water for purity, boundary, and beauty. You can follow your intuition here, as long as your intention to cleanse and purify is clear and at the forefront of your mind.

Along with a grounding meditation, cleansing is the perfect way to begin your ritual craft because it allows you to start with a blank slate, enhancing the potency of your focus and the power of your tools. While you are cleansing, you can envision negative energy being banished while strong energetic boundaries arise to protect your space. As you end your cleanse, you can begin to bring your focus to your intention for your ritual and visualize the effects to come. If you do not start out with purification, you could incorporate unwanted emotions, energies, and even spirits into your spell or ritual. The result could be anything from the spell lacking potency to generating chaos in your life to potentially opening yourself up to dangerous energies.

Useful Tools in Appalachian Folk Magic

Appalachian witches incorporate many tools into their practices. From brooms to cauldrons to candles, having magical tools at your fingertips can elevate your craft. Often, a single tool can be used for many different magical purposes. While it can certainly enhance your practice to have an arsenal of tools at the ready, you can also transform household objects into magical allies as needed.

For example, you could use a pair of kitchen scissors to harvest herbs instead of a crescent boline (a ritual knife) and still have the same outcome: wild foraged herbs for your ritual. However, I have found that when I have dedicated tools, it tends to generate a sense of witchy excitement within me! So even if you don't have the classic boline for harvesting, having a dedicated set of shears for magical harvests can be beneficial—especially when you're cleansing yourself, your space, and your tools before beginning.

Don't feel pressured to buy every single magical tool you can think of, but here are a few to add to your wish list and get you started on your journey. Each of the following tools serves multiple purposes and can be used to enhance the potency of your workings.

Mortar and Pestle

A mortar and pestle is a tool dating back to the Stone Age that is used to crush herbs or resins into fine powders and combine them into a powerful mixture for your spells. The set is essentially a bowl and a small "club," and the club is used to grind the herbs against the bowl. Some modern practitioners, especially those who produce high-volume products for purchase, use blenders or coffee grinders instead of a mortar and pestle. However, I find that working hands-on with your spell ingredients in this way strengthens your intention and the power of the herbs.

Broom

Technically speaking, any broom can be designated for magical use, but I recommend investing in two different types of brooms for your Appalachian witchcraft practice. The first is either a full-size sweeper broom, or a besom, made with a solid branch handle and broomcorn bristles. This broom can be used to sweep your floors and the corners of your home when you are doing energetic cleansing or tidying up before or after a spell. The second is a handheld whisk, or "turkey wing," broom, and this one is meant for sweeping off smaller surfaces and cleansing your altar space.

Candles

Candles are an essential part of many witches' magical practice, and candle magic is covered in more detail in chapter 10. There are many different types of candles with various magical uses. "Chime" or "spell" candles are narrow, colored candles that are about four inches long. Tea lights are small, shallow candles, usually enclosed in metal. Both chime candles and tea lights are typically used in shorter-term spells. Pillar candles vary in size and are usually lit over the course of a few days for longer-term rituals. Seven-day candles are pillar candles enclosed in glass, typically used over the course of a week.

TIME YOUR SPELLS CAREFULLY

You can imagine that the timing of your spell is an ingredient in and of itself. When your working is timed properly, matching the significance of the time with the intention of your spell, you can significantly enhance its potency. There are many different ways to go about timing your spells effectively.

One way is through understanding the planetary rulers of each day of the week. Monday is ruled by the moon, enhancing intuition and the goddess. Tuesday is associated with Mars, so this is a day for fiery action. Mercury rules Wednesday, empowering communication and meditative work. Thursday is Jupiter's day—great for abundance and exploration. Friday is under Venus's influence, making it the perfect day for love and beauty magic. Saturn rules Saturday, so this is a great day for boundary work. Finally, Sunday is the sun's day, powerful for manifestation, shedding light, and self-expression. Sunday is also considered a sacred day in Christianity. Sometimes called a day of rest, Sunday is also a good day to do "the Lord's work," so in the realm of Appalachian witchcraft, it's a day for faith-based healing.

The time of day can also enhance your workings. Sunrise and the morning hours are a great time to work magic around new beginnings and to shed light on a problem. High noon brings balance and justice. Sunset and the evening hours are a perfect time for closing chapters, cord cutting, and banishment.

Some witches celebrate the sabbats—the holidays that mark the wheel of the year: Samhain (October 31–November 1), Yule (winter solstice, December 21–23), Imbolc (February 1–2), Ostara (spring equinox, March 19–22), Beltane (May 1), Litha (summer solstice, June 19–22), Lughnasadh (August 1), and Mabon (September 19–23). Seasonal rituals performed on these days are enhanced by the magic of the holiday.

Cauldron

Cauldrons are one of the first things I recommend sourcing for your magical journey. Not only are they practical fire-safe vessels that serve many purposes, but their innate affiliation with witchcraft adds a mystical aura to any spell. Cauldrons are made of cast iron, and they can be used to burn loose incense, create small ritual fires, and craft black salts (which are covered in chapter 8). Cauldrons come in a few different sizes. I recommend the smaller ones for burning incense and the larger ones (five inches in diameter or more) for fires and black salts.

Boline

A boline is a ritual knife, typically used for harvesting herbs and carving candles. You can also use bolines in cord-cutting rituals. Classic bolines have a white handle and a crescent moon blade, but these days there are many options on the market. I recommend sourcing a boline that comes with a sheath, both for storage and for safety. While you can absolutely substitute scissors for a boline, there is something rather magical about harvesting herbs with this tool. I personally feel a deeper connection to the land and to the witches of the past when I use mine.

Draw Power from the Earth and Sky

The Appalachian witchcraft tradition is innately a nature-based path. So much of this folk magic practice is centered around the messages and resources the earth generously provides. Collecting ingredients for your spellwork directly from nature, when done responsibly, can be such a potent part of your magical practice. Appalachian witches made use of the magical allies that surrounded them, like soils, waters, stones, and more. Even if you don't live in the Appalachian region, I still encourage you to collect as many ingredients from your natural surroundings as you can, being mindful not to overharvest or trespass, so that it is a sustainable practice.

Sourcing your ingredients in this way deepens your connection to the earth and your immediate environment, which is a powerful way to enhance your magical workings. In a way, the foraging process becomes a part of the spell itself, allowing you to manifest your intention every step of the way. Although it is convenient, and perfectly acceptable, to acquire your ingredients by purchasing them, when you can forage them yourself, it brings you into deeper connection with the original Appalachian witches, who often only worked with what they could immediately access in their natural surroundings.

When working with the land, it is also important to consider its Indigenous history. The land you live on is loved, revered, and nurtured by Indigenous people, and in acts of supreme violence, that relationship was severed. Knowing the history of the land and doing your part to contribute to land healing is an important facet of Appalachian witchcraft. This can be done by supporting land-back movements, learning about the history of the land, and turning to Indigenous communities for leadership.

Churchyard Dirt

Churchyard dirt, best collected on a Sunday, has traditionally been used in many types of spells and rituals. Primarily used in healing or curative workings, churchyard dirt can also be used in spells for purification, protection, and strengthening relationships. Because the church is seen as holy ground, the dirt from the property is imbued with that energy. You will want to use caution when collecting churchyard dirt. While there are many churches that do not mind at all, there are some, especially in the Bible Belt, that would not take kindly to a witch collecting their soils for a spell.

Rainwater

Rainwater also has many magical uses, including purification, cleansing, and increasing psychic and emotional intuition. When collecting rainwater, choose a clean vessel that you have also purified energetically. Then place it outside either before or during a storm, making sure that its opening has a clear view of the sky above. You don't want to collect water that is dripping off of a roof or a tree because the water will contain dirt and debris, which negates the purifying effects. I recommend only using rainwater topically and in spells, not ingesting it.

Salt

Salt is often used in protection and purification magic, and it is one of the ingredients that it is certainly easiest to buy. However, you can actually extract your own salts by following these instructions. First, dig up a handful of dandelion roots and rinse them thoroughly. Boil them in just enough water to submerge the roots. Once the water turns dark, carefully scoop out the roots. Continue to boil until all the water has evaporated. At the bottom of your pot, there will be a thin layer of black or gray substance, a mixture of salt and other trace minerals.

Red Clay

Red clay is abundant in Appalachia. In fact, if you dig on pretty much any plot of undeveloped, unfarmed land in the Blue Ridge Mountains, you will find red clay. Clay has, of course, been used in terra cotta pottery for centuries, but it also has magical uses. It is grounding and cooling in nature and is also thought to draw out toxins. It can be used as body paint during rituals. It also has a connection to the element of fire, so it can be used to evoke that element in a spell without the use of a literal flame.

Morning Dew

Morning dew can be used in beauty magic as well as cleansing spells. To collect dew, take a bowl outside first thing in the morning and shake plant life over it, allowing the dew drops to collect in the bowl. The dew can then be transferred into a smaller vessel or used immediately in your spell. You can also use the dew while it is still on a plant, as the dew will amplify the energy of that ally. For example, if you use the dew collected on a rosebud, it would be perfect for love and beauty magic.

Useful Herbs in Appalachian Witchcraft

There are numerous herbs that grow wild in the Appalachian region that lend themselves to magical and curative workings. Although we now live in a world where it is easy to access herbs that are native to other areas of the world, the original Appalachian witches were inclined to use what was naturally available to them in their workings. Luckily, these mountains are home to an abundance of herbs, and even if you do not live in the region, these herbs are common across many parts of the world.

If you are able to forage your herbs or find and harvest them out in nature, a general rule of thumb is to only collect 10 percent of the herb that is readily available. This is how we can sustainably wildcraft and ensure that we do not kill off the local plant life. Of course, when you are harvesting your own plants, you can follow your own intuition, but I still like to follow the 10 percent rule so that my plants continue to thrive for years.

Here are a few of the herbs that have been used throughout the Appalachian folk magic tradition, along with their magical and curative uses.

Witch Hazel

Today, we are perhaps most familiar with witch hazel extract, which, due to its astringent properties, can be used to treat minor skin ailments like bug bites, scrapes, and blemishes. This extract is crafted by soaking the roots of witch hazel in 40 percent alcohol for at least two weeks, straining it, and adding an equal amount of distilled water. Witch hazel has also been used for divination. Its Y-shaped branches have been used to dowse for water, and its flowers have been used in herbal sachets to increase psychic ability and access higher wisdom.

Dandelion

On a physical level, the antioxidant- and vitamin-rich dandelion has been used for cleansing the liver and even as an anti-inflammatory. Magically, the dandelion is affiliated with the sun and is therefore used in abundance and manifestation magic. It can also be used in banishment and transformation rituals, and it is known to increase psychic powers, especially through our dreams. As children, we probably all took part in a dandelion ritual—picking a seed-filled dandelion, making a wish, and blowing the seeds into the wind. It is believed that as those seeds germinate and grow, so do our desires.

Peppermint

The mint family contains many powerful allies, like spearmint, lemon balm, catnip, bee balm, and more, that are all abundant in the Appalachian region, but peppermint is likely the most well-known. In curative workings, peppermint is used to settle the digestive system, alleviate symptoms of anxiety, and promote sleep. Magically, peppermint is affiliated with wealth and luck. This is because of mint's abundant nature; if you plant it in a garden bed, it will take over unless you diligently harvest it. Peppermint can be used in protection and purification rituals, and it's a common ingredient in love workings as well.

Mugwort

Mugwort is known for its potency in meditation, dream work, and astral projection. It activates our psychic centers and can also be used for energetic protection and to shield the mind. On a physical level, mugwort is a bitter herb that has been used to settle the stomach and cleanse the body of toxins, as it supports liver function. It is important to note that mugwort is an emmenagogue, which means that it can stimulate menstruation in those with uteruses. This means that if you are pregnant, it is not advised to use this herb, as it could cause complications.

Wild Violets

Wild violets are one of my favorite seasonal herbs to use in my workings. They have heart-shaped leaves and white and purple petals, and they bloom in springtime. Every part of the wild violet plant is edible, making them a colorful addition to your springtime diet—but be careful to forage in an area where pesticides aren't used. Wild violets are packed with vitamins and antioxidants and, when used in tea, can be used to soothe respiratory issues. Associated with the planet Venus, wild violet is a powerful ally in love and beauty magic, as well as boosting luck and peace of mind.

GROW YOUR OWN HERB GARDEN

Growing your own herbs is a powerful way to connect with the earth, your power, and the plants you will be using in your spellwork. It is also an excellent solution for witches without access to forage wild herbs. When you grow your own magical ingredients, you can raise them with magical intentions in mind. You can enchant them as they grow and even bury written charms in the soil.

Rosemary, garden sage, basil, thyme, peppermint, and oregano are hardy in most growing conditions and easy to care for. Rosemary is ideal for protection and working with the ancestors. Garden sage is a variety of sage that thrives in many regions and has protective and purifying qualities. Basil can be used for psychic activation, easing the mind, and attracting wealth. Thyme is used in healing spells and to encourage peace of mind. Peppermint is great for settling the stomach and generating abundance. Oregano has incredible healing power and has also been used for navigating legal troubles and calming the nervous system.

These plants do best outside with partial sunlight, but they can also be grown indoors in bright, indirect light, as long as you're sure not to under- or overwater. If you do choose to plant them outside, with great care, these plants will return each spring, after a winter's rest. Either way, developing a relationship with these herbal allies in this way is sure to enhance your magical practice.

Give Thanks to the Earth and Its Gifts

To live in right relationship with the earth, we should be giving as much as we are receiving. So each time you forage materials for your spellwork, you should offer something in return. Whether it is a prayer, an offering of water or a crystal, or simply a moment of gratitude, intention is key—giving your thanks for what you've received. For example, when I am harvesting herbs, I like to bring a watering can with me, with rose quartz in the water. When I am done harvesting from a plant, I pour the water onto the plant I harvested from and thank the plant and the earth for the abundance it offered me.

We should also forage with a deep sense of reverence. Even though we now have tools that can harvest quickly and recklessly, taking our time and moving with care is another way to express our gratitude to the earth. Instead of harvesting an herb in massive quantities, take your time to select the individual flowers, leaves, or stems that are calling out to you. In addition to following the 10 percent rule for foraging, it's also important to be mindful of how much you need or can make use of. However, if you ever do overharvest for a spell, you always have the option to save those materials for a future working. Herbs can be preserved by hanging them upside down to dry and then storing them in airtight containers once they are completely dried.

Key Takeaways

In this chapter, you have learned about many tools and natural ingredients you can incorporate into your craft to enhance your magic and honor the origins of Appalachian magic.

◆ Part of the fun of practicing magic is exploring new methods and learning what resonates through your own experience.

◆ Along with a grounding meditation, cleansing is the perfect way to begin your ritual craft because it allows you to start with a blank slate, enhancing the potency of your focus and the power of your tools.

◆ Appalachian witches incorporate many tools into their practice. From brooms to cauldrons to candles, having magical tools at your fingertips can elevate your craft.

◆ Appalachian witches have traditionally made use of the magical allies that surrounded them, like soils, waters, stones, and more. Even if you don't live in the Appalachian region, try to collect as many ingredients from your natural surroundings as possible, being mindful not to overharvest or trespass, so that it is a sustainable practice.

◆ To live in right relationship with the earth, we should be giving as much as we are receiving. Each time we forage materials for our spellwork, we should be offering something in return.

PART II

PRACTICING APPALACHIAN WITCHCRAFT

Now that you have established a solid foundational understanding of Appalachian folk magic, it is time for you to begin your work as an Appalachian witch! Part 2 of this book serves as an initiatory book of spells, guiding you through the magical realms that are critical to the Appalachian witchcraft practice. In this section, you will find spells to strengthen your connection to the earth, heal with the power of nature, cleanse yourself and your space, support your personal relationships, protect what you deem sacred, craft poppets, work candle magic, and even divine the future.

As you work through the spells shared here, I highly recommend keeping your own grimoire, or book of spells. To start, choose a spell that's calling out to you and begin to follow it as it is written. As you work the spell, use your grimoire to note any intuitive changes you may make and the steps you are following. Once the spell is complete, you can make note of any feelings that arose throughout the process and what you sensed upon its completion. This is an incredible way to witness your own journey as a witch, and it helps you re-create the spell in the future!

CHAPTER 4

Strengthen Your Connection with the Land

Deepening your connection to the earth is a great way to start your journey into Appalachian folk magic. In this chapter, you will learn a handful of ways to strengthen your connection to the land through rituals, meditations, charms, and more. Many of the practices included in this chapter can be especially helpful if you integrate them on a regular basis—even daily.

You will learn how to ground and intertwine your energy with the earth itself, call upon the earthen spirits, and honor the earth as a living ancestor. These are core practices in this folk magic craft, because our relationship with the earth is one of the most important aspects of Appalachian witchcraft. If you feel particularly drawn to this kind of earth-based magic, be sure to check out the Resources section (page 144) for recommendations to dive deeper into this realm.

By the end of this chapter, you should have a strong groundwork for earth-based spellwork as you journey deeper into magic. These foundational methodologies can be returned to throughout your practice to bring you back to the roots of Appalachian witchcraft: living in deep connection with the earth.

GROUNDING INTO THE EARTH'S ENERGY

This meditation can be used while you are out in nature or from the comfort of your own home. As you ground into the energy of the earth, you deepen your relationship with this planet and nature itself. This meditation is a great way to start and end your day. The more you practice this meditation, the deeper your connection to the earth may grow.

TIME: 10 to 15 minutes

MATERIALS

A comfortable place to sit

1. Once you're seated comfortably, close your eyes and begin to physically ground with your body: lengthen your spine, and if you are sitting in a chair, plant your feet on the ground.

2. Bring your awareness to your breath. Allow your stomach to expand with each inhale and contract with each exhale. Envision that with each exhale, you are releasing all the tension in your body.

3. Now, bring your focus to your root, right at the base of your spine. With each exhale, envision golden roots spreading from the base of your spine and growing downward into the ground.

4. With each exhale, imagine these roots growing deeper, tunneling through all the different layers of the earth—through the mineral-rich soils and past crystalline caverns and water reservoirs. All along the way, your root system is enchanted by the magic within the earth.

CONTINUED →

5. With a deep exhale, envision these golden roots reaching the center of the wise earth.

6. Now, with each inhale, visualize that you are drawing up energy from the center of the earth through your golden, shimmering roots. With each inhale, understand that this earthen wisdom is guided back up and into your body.

7. With a deep inhale, let this earthen energy land fully in your heart. As you exhale, allow this wisdom to anchor in your body, integrating as embodied truth. With another deep breath, open your eyes.

CANDLE DRESSING FOR EARTHEN CONNECTION

"Dressing a candle" refers to infusing a candle with intention and energy from oils, stones, and herbs. In this ritual, you will be creating a candle to strengthen your connection to the earth. This candle can be used on your earthen altar or burned over the course of seven days.

TIME: 20 minutes, plus overnight to charge

MATERIALS

Small dish

1 tablespoon olive oil

4 or 5 drops essential oils of your choice

1 teaspoon dried rosemary

Carving tool (toothpick, knife, etc.)

1 green or brown pillar candle

Small spoon

1. In the small dish, combine the olive oil, essential oils, and rosemary and allow the mixture to infuse while you perform the next steps.

2. Next, use your carving tool to carve patterns, designs, or words into the candle. For example, on one side you could inscribe "CONNECT," and on the other, you could carve "EARTH." You will want to create a fair number of grooves in the top and sides of the candle for the oils and herbs. If your candle is in a glass jar, you will be focused on dressing the top of the candle only. If your candle has bare sides, you can dress the top as well as the sides.

CONTINUED →

3. Use the small spoon to pour your infused oil onto the top and sides of the candle, then use your fingers to rub the oil and herbs into the grooves of your candle. While you are doing this, focus your intention on connecting deeply with the earth.

4. Allow your candle to sit overnight, preferably in a moonlit window.

5. Now your candle can be used in altar work. If your candle is not enclosed in glass, be sure that you burn it in a fire-safe dish. Always supervise your candle as it burns.

CREATE AN ALTAR TO THE LAND

A great way to nurture a connection to the land is by creating an altar to the earth in your sacred space. This allows you to work with the land's energy even if you cannot spend time in nature each day. This is a lifesaver if you live in an urban or suburban area where you don't have regular access to untamed nature. Enhance this practice by learning the original names of the land and the peoples who lived on it. Check the Resources section (page 144) for guidance.

TIME: 30 to 45 minutes

MATERIALS

Natural items collected from outside

1 green or brown candle

Candle holder

Vessel for water

Fire-safe dish

Rosemary or cedar burning bundle

Lighter or matches

1. First, responsibly collect items from nature that call out to you. Some of my favorites are pine cones, lichen-covered twigs, and mossy rocks.

2. Once you have collected your items from nature, begin to set up the main features of your altar: the candle in the candle holder, the vessel for water, and the fire-safe dish, with the burning bundle inside.

3. Next, start to decorate the altar with the items collected from outside, ensuring that nothing flammable is too close to the candle or the fire-safe dish.

CONTINUED →

4. Fill your vessel with water. Spring water or rainwater is preferred if you have access to these. You can even place natural items in the water if you desire.

5. Once the altar is set, take a moment with both palms raised toward the altar and meditate. You can even use the grounding meditation from earlier in the chapter (page 51).

6. Now light the candle. As you do, say aloud, "With this altar, I honor my connection to this sacred land."

7. Use the candle's flame to light the tip of your rosemary or cedar burning bundle. Both of these herbs call on the earth ancestors for protection and guidance.

8. Return to your altar often to strengthen your connection to the land by lighting another candle, continuing to burn your burning bundle, or simply meditating in front of it.

CALL UPON THE SPIRIT OF THE LAND

This spell is meant to help you connect with the spirit(s) of the land you live on. As always, when calling on spirits, you want to be sure that you are calling on loving, good-natured energy. Be sure that you have cleansed, grounded, and protected your energy before working this spell.

TIME: 20 to 30 minutes

MATERIALS

Natural items collected from outside

Glass of spring water

1. First, take a walk in your natural surroundings. Keeping your intention to connect with the spirit of the land in mind, keep an eye out for any natural items that intuitively speak to you. These are meant to enhance your connection to spirit.

2. Once you feel complete with your walk and have collected enough items, you can either return home or, if it is safe and accessible, find a nice spot to sit on the land.

3. Place the glass of spring water in front of you, along with the natural items you foraged.

4. Close your eyes and start with a grounding meditation (page 51). Once you feel grounded, proceed.

CONTINUED →

5. Say aloud, "I call upon the loving spirit of this land for guidance, wisdom, and intuition." Hold that intention in your heart. Feel out whether you feel a connection forming or if you should state your intention aloud again. Repeat if needed.

6. Next, state aloud, "I am open to working in right relationship with the loving spirit of this land." Again, use your intuition before proceeding and repeat if needed.

7. Open your eyes and pick up your glass of spring water. Speaking directly into the water, say, "I now embody my connection to the loving spirit of this land." Drink the glass of water entirely.

8. Seal the spell by stating, "I walk in peaceful connection with the loving spirit of this land."

CARRY THE EARTH'S ENERGY WITH YOU

Use this spell to charm a piece of jewelry or something else that you can wear daily to enhance your connection with the earth. It's best to use something you feel a personal connection to already.

TIME: 20 minutes, plus 7 days to charge, plus 10 minutes to complete

MATERIALS

Jar of soil

Writing utensil

Slip of paper

Piece of jewelry or something else you can wear daily

6 inches string or twine

1 flower or leaf

Lighter or matches

Fire-safe dish

1. Start by collecting a jar of soil from the land. Make sure the jar is big enough to also hold the item you are charming.

2. Next, write down your intention on the slip of paper. It could be something like "This ring represents my unending connection to the earth." Use your intuition here and remember your intention for later.

3. Place your item in the center of the slip of paper. Fold the item into the paper, being sure that it is completely covered. Wrap and tie the twine to keep the paper in place.

4. Next, bury the enclosed item in the jar of soil. Place your flower or leaf on top once your item is buried.

CONTINUED →

5. Holding the jar in your hand, repeat the intention you wrote on your slip of paper.

6. Place the jar of soil on a windowsill for 7 days.

7. After 7 days, unbury the parcel. Untie the twine, repeating your intention.

8. Put your item on, repeating your intention.

9. Finally, seal the spell by burning your slip of paper over a fire-safe dish as you state your intention a final time.

10. Charge your item in this way any time you feel called to refresh it.

HERBAL SACHET TO HONOR
THE EARTH ANCESTORS

This sachet can be placed under your pillow or on your altar to deepen your connection to the earth ancestors. You can crush the herbs between your fingers to renew the scent. Whenever the scent disappears, you know it is time to refresh the herbs. The stones can be reused as well.

TIME: 20 minutes

MATERIALS

Small dish

2 small rose quartz pieces

2 small aragonite pieces

1 tablespoon dried sage

1 tablespoon dried peppermint

1 tablespoon dried rosemary

1 tablespoon dried rose petals

1 tablespoon dried thyme

Small spoon

Cloth or organza drawstring
  sachet

1. Place the small dish, centered, in front of you. On the left side, place one rose quartz and one aragonite. These two stones will represent the earth. On the right side, place the other two stones, to represent yourself.

2. Add the sage, peppermint, rosemary, rose, and thyme to the small dish one at a time, calling on them by name and intention: "Sage for clarity and protection. Peppermint for luck. Rosemary to honor the ancestors. Rose for divine love. Thyme for health and psychic connection."

3. Use the spoon to mix the herbs together, stirring in a clockwise motion to attract energy.

CONTINUED →

4. As you stir, say aloud, "I deepen my connection to the loving earth ancestors."

5. Hold the dish up to your nose and gently inhale the fragrance. State the intention aloud once more.

6. Using the spoon, begin to transfer the herbs into your sachet. With each spoonful, keep your intention in your mind.

7. Once the sachet is filled with the herbal mixture, add the stones from the left side of the dish and say, "These stones represent the loving earth ancestors."

8. Next, add the stones from the right and say, "These stones represent me. Together, they represent my connection to the loving earth ancestors."

9. Finally, tie the herbal sachet closed.

CHAPTER 5

Heal with the Power of Nature

Working with the healing power of nature is a crucial facet of Appalachian witchcraft. In this chapter, you will learn a few magical curative remedies and rituals that make use of powerful herbal and crystal allies. You will also activate your intuition, open as a healing channel, and learn how to make each meal a healing ceremony.

The following rituals and meditations will guide you as you begin your magical healing journey, and as you progress with your magic, you can start to use some of these spells and skills to assist your loved ones as well. Remember, while most original Appalachian witches were solitary practitioners, meaning they practiced their craft alone, they often held important roles in society. Although as witches and not medical professionals we cannot offer true medical advice, our herbal wisdom and remedies can certainly benefit those around us.

This collection of spells and remedies will teach you how to soothe a sore throat, mend a broken heart, exude a youthful glow, and more. As you incorporate these rituals into your practice, remember to keep your intuitive channel open and allow them to evolve alongside you.

OPEN THE HEALING CHANNEL

This meditation will guide you in connecting with your body and the curative remedies it may need. This can be a great start to the day, and you can plan your meals and beverages around what your body is seeking.

TIME: 15 minutes

MATERIALS

Notebook   Writing utensil

1. Start with a grounding meditation (page 51).

2. Once you finish the grounding meditation, bring your awareness to the very top of your head and slowly lower your inner gaze down into your skull, your brain, your forehead, down into your face, your neck, and your throat. All the while, take note of any discomfort, pressure, or tension that may be present.

3. Continue this full-body scan, spreading to your shoulders, your arms, your hands, and your fingers. Then, bring attention to your chest, your heart, your stomach, your digestive system, and your pelvis.

4. Next, bring attention to your spinal column, then down each leg to the feet and the toes.

5. Take a moment here to sense what is calling out for healing. If you need to, you can write these things down now. If you can remember them, keep your eyes closed and proceed.

6. Now, bringing your focus to your crown, to your mind's eye, ask for healing wisdom to move through your body as a channel, to lead you to the remedies that will soothe your ailments.

7. If you haven't already, write down the areas of your body you sensed are in need of healing in step 5. Now take an intuitive pass over these items and write down any remedies that you remember. For example, you've learned peppermint can help settle a sour stomach.

8. If you need to, turn to books or online resources to help you craft curative remedies and healing meals.

HEART-HEALING RITUAL BATH

This ritual helps energetically heal the heart, whether you are feeling heartbroken or you're just in need of some extra love magic.

TIME: 45 minutes

MATERIALS

Small dish

2 tablespoons dried rose petals

2 tablespoons dried hibiscus

2 tablespoons dried peppermint

1 cinnamon stick

Small spoon

Cloth or organza drawstring
 sachet

1 small or large rose quartz piece

Bathtub

1. In the small dish, combine the rose petals, hibiscus, and peppermint. As you add each herb, call them by name and intention: "Rose for divine love. Hibiscus for opening and healing the heart. Peppermint for good fortune and love.

2. Stir the mixture clockwise with the cinnamon stick calling it by name and intention: "Cinnamon for passion, magic, and warming the heart."

3. Next, while still stirring, state your intention over the herbal mixture. It can be something like, "My heart is open, healed, and loving."

4. With your intention in mind, begin placing your ingredients in the sachet, adding the cinnamon stick first and then spooning in the herbal mixture. If your piece of rose quartz is small enough to place in the bag, you can put that in last. Otherwise, you can add it to the bath later. Tie the sachet closed.

5. Begin running warm or hot water in the bathtub. As you place the rose quartz and sachet into the bathwater, repeat your intention.

6. As you step into the bath, repeat your intention again, either silently in your mind or aloud.

7. Once the tub is filled, if the water is not deep enough to submerge your heart-center, flip over onto your stomach so that the water reaches your chest.

8. Bring your attention to your intention and state it aloud.

9. Clear your mind and settle into silence. See if any intuitive messages come through for continued heart healing.

REJUVENATE WITH BEAUTY MAGIC

This remedy combines the healing powers of multiple herbal allies to create an herbal toner that will promote glowing, clear skin. If you have sensitive skin, you may want to do a patch test to ensure that you will not have an adverse reaction. Because this is beauty magic, it's best to create the toner on a Friday and allow it to brew until the following Friday. Friday is ruled by Venus, the planet of love and beauty.

TIME: 10 minutes, plus 7 days to brew, plus 10 minutes to complete

MATERIALS

1 (32-ounce) mason jar

3 tablespoons dried calendula

2 tablespoons dried rose petals

1 tablespoon dried lemon balm

1 (16-ounce) bottle witch hazel

Fine mesh strainer

Liquid measuring cup

Label

Permanent marker

1. In your mason jar, combine your herbal allies (calendula, rose petals, and lemon balm), calling them by name and intention: "Calendula for a healing glow. Rose to soothe the skin. Lemon balm for rejuvenation."

2. Next, pour the entire bottle of witch hazel onto the herbal mixture, calling it by name and intention: "Witch hazel for cleansing, clearing, and healing." Save the bottle if you wish.

3. Now close the jar and place it in a cool, dark cabinet for 7 or more days. Check on your brew once a day and affirm its intention—something like, "Glowing, radiant skin mirroring beauty within."

4. After your toner is finished brewing, strain it into a liquid measuring cup.

5. You can pour the strained toner either back into the original bottle or into a clean mason jar. Either way, label your creation with its title, ingredient list, and the date of creation.

6. You can use this facial toner daily as a quick and accessible way to incorporate beauty magic into your everyday life.

SOOTHING TEA FOR A SORE THROAT

This herbal tea is the perfect ally for a sore throat or for any time you feel your communication is blocked. These herbs support the throat on both a physical and an energetic level. The ingredients in this soothing tea have been shown to reduce the risk of infection, fight bacteria, thin and clear mucus in the throat, and soothe soreness.

TIME: 15 minutes

MATERIALS

Small pot

2 cups water

1 inch ginger root, chopped

½ lemon

1 tablespoon apple cider vinegar

Fine mesh strainer

Mug

2 tablespoons local honey, plus more to taste

Small spoon

1. In a small pot, bring the water to a boil over high heat.

2. Once it is boiling, add the ginger. Call it by name and intention: "Ginger for clearing and soothing my throat." Allow it to boil for one minute, then remove the pot from the heat.

3. Set a timer for 2 to 3 minutes. While you wait, squeeze the lemon into the pot. Say, "Lemon for boosting immunity."

4. Add the apple cider vinegar. Say, "Apple cider vinegar for ridding my throat of toxins."

5. When the timer goes off, strain the tea into the mug.

6. Add the honey and say, "Honey for calming and soothing."

7. Use the spoon to stir in the honey counterclockwise to banish soreness, infection, and blockages in this energy center. Add more honey to taste if you wish.

8. Speak your intention into your mug of healing tea. If your throat is physically sore, maybe your intention is something like, "This tea soothes and heals my sore throat." If you are calling on these allies to clear your throat energetically and activate clear communication, you may say something like, "This tea supports me as I speak my truth freely and clearly."

9. Enjoy your curative remedy!

"LET FOOD BE THY MEDICINE": INTENTIONAL MEAL PREP

There is an old saying: "Let food be thy medicine, and medicine be thy food." You do not have to wait for the perfect herbal remedy to begin a healing journey. You can cook meals that support your body's needs physically, energetically, and medicinally and imbue them with the magical power of intention.

TIME: 15 to 20 minutes before cooking a meal, plus cook time

MATERIALS

Ingredients for the meal you're cooking

Books or online resources about your ingredients

1. Gather the ingredients for the meal you are cooking, including spices and herbs.

2. As you wash your produce, visualize each item being cleansed both physically and energetically.

3. Go through each item and determine what properties it will add to your meal. For example, garlic is great for the heart, bones, and immune system. If you need to, turn to books or online resources.

4. Practice the "Open the Healing Channel" meditation (page 64). Notice the ways you've already intuitively chosen foods that resonate with your body's needs. See if you are called to add any other ingredients after checking in with your body in this way.

5. After considering all of the benefits of your ingredients, determine an intention for the meal. For example, a hot and sour soup recipe I make often is intended to boost the immune system and clear out stuck energy.

6. As you continue to prep your ingredients and begin cooking your meal, keep this intention in mind. You can even call each ingredient out by name and intention.

7. As you cook, align your stirring motion with your intention. Counterclockwise stirring is meant to banish energy, so if you're getting rid of a cold, counterclockwise motion is perfect. Clockwise stirring is meant to call in energy.

8. Once the meal is prepared, say a prayer aloud over the food that speaks to the intention of the meal. Enjoy!

ELIXIR FOR A CALM MIND

This elixir can be brewed as a tea or added to bathwater to calm the mind and soothe the nervous system. Tulsi has been known to lower cortisol levels in the body, while lavender promotes healthy sleep cycles and eases stress. Amethyst is known as a stone of relaxation. Together, these earthen allies will help you unwind from the day.

TIME: 15 minutes

MATERIALS

Medium pot

2 cups water

2 tablespoons dried tulsi (holy basil)

2 tablespoons dried lavender

1 small amethyst

Fine mesh strainer

Mug (if drinking elixir)

Honey to taste (if drinking elixir)

Bathtub (if taking a ritual bath)

1. In a medium pot, bring the water to a boil over high heat.

2. Once the water is boiling, add the tulsi and lavender. Call them by name and intention: "Tulsi to reduce stress. Lavender to promote rest."

3. Remove the pot from the heat and set a timer for 4 minutes. As the water steams, speak your intentions into the herbal remedy. Your intention could be something like, "These allies lull me into restful, dreamy sleep" or "Lavender and tulsi reduce my stress and help me unwind."

4. As the tea continues to steep, thoroughly wash the amethyst with soap and water. Rinse well, intending that the water cleanses the stone both physically and energetically. Add it to the mug. Call it by name and intention: "Amethyst for relaxation."

5. Once the time is up, strain the herbal elixir into the mug.

6. If you are drinking this elixir as a tea, add honey to taste and stir clockwise to call in your intention. Speak your intention aloud as you stir.

7. If you are using this elixir in a ritual bath, run your bathwater and pour the elixir into the tub in a clockwise motion to call in your intention. Speak your intention aloud as you pour.

CHAPTER 6

Cleanse Your Space of Impurities

As we learned in chapter 1, everything we do or say within a space leaves an energetic imprint behind. Then, when we take other people, animals, world events, and the spirit realm into account, we are left with quite a lot of energy that we may not want lingering in our space. Cleansing rituals are the perfect way to wipe the slate clean and start anew.

With a regular cleansing practice, you may find yourself living in a more peaceful atmosphere, having a calmer mind, and getting deeper sleep. Negative energy can be draining on a physical and energetic level. Keeping the energy of your sacred space clear, within and without, is sometimes called "energetic hygiene." Often, witches see these practices as important as mundane hygienic practices, like bathing or brushing your teeth.

In this chapter, you'll learn multiple ways to cleanse and clear your mind, your body, and your space of any unwanted energy. Cleansing and protection magic are often similar in nature, and you will learn more about bold protection spells in chapter 8. For now, we will focus on cleansing negative energy and keeping your space clear. These rituals and meditations will help you develop a strong purification practice.

CREATING SACRED SPACE
IN THE MIND

This meditation is a great way to start any cleansing ritual. It will help ground you into your power, rid you of negative energy you may be holding on to, and clear the way to continue in a deeper cleansing ceremony.

TIME: 15 minutes

MATERIALS

A quiet space with no distractions

1. Start by finding a comfortable place to sit or lie down and close your eyes.

2. Bring your attention to your breath, allowing the energetic breath to cascade down the front and back of the heart. As you exhale, envision tension leaving your body and spirit.

3. After taking a few deep breaths in this way, bring your focus to your toes and your feet and envision all negative energy being swept away.

4. Work your way up the body like this, bringing attention to the legs, the hips, the stomach, the chest, the arms, the hands, and the fingers. Then focus on the neck and the face, and finally, rest your attention on the mind.

5. Notice any negative thoughts that surface as you rest your focus on the mind. Imagine those thoughts being whisked away by your breath.

CONTINUED →

6. Now state the following intention aloud: "My mind is clear. My being is a sacred space." Continue to breathe into this intention.

7. Give yourself a few thoughtless moments, however long it takes to reach that quiet-minded place. Once you feel complete, repeat your intention aloud.

8. Then, cover your eyelids with your hands and take a deep inhale. As you exhale, open your eyes under your palms, then slowly move your hands away from your eyes. This will allow the light to slowly trickle into your awareness.

9. Finally, take your time grounding back into the physical realm. From here, you can continue with a cleansing ritual or go about your day.

CLEANSE AND CLEAR YOUR SPACE

This cleansing ritual is the perfect follow-up to the previous meditation ("Creating Sacred Space in the Mind," page 77). This ritual will help you "wipe the slate clean," so to speak, and can be performed as frequently as needed. The use of burning herbs and feathers or wings to cleanse space has roots in certain Indigenous practices, like the ceremonies of Turtle Island.

TIME: 20 to 30 minutes

MATERIALS

Fire-safe dish
Dried rosemary bundle
  (for burning)

Lighter or matches
Feather or wing fan

1. If you are able, start by opening all the windows and doors. This allows an outlet for the negative energy—otherwise, you are stirring energy up and giving it nowhere to go!

2. If you are working in a space that has multiple floors, you can start either on the very bottom or very top floor. I prefer to work in a counterclockwise motion to banish negative energy.

3. Once you decide where to start, place the fire-safe dish in front of you, holding the rosemary bundle in your nondominant hand. Using your dominant hand, light the tip of the bundle, calling the ally by name and intention: "Rosemary to help clear, cleanse, and protect this sacred space."

4. Pick up your feather with your dominant hand. It will be used to direct the smoke.

CONTINUED →

5. Place the bundle in the fire-safe dish and pick it up in your non-dominant hand. Begin to fan the smoke with your feather. As you do, repeat your intention—something like, "Only love remains."

6. Use the feather to guide the smoke into the corners of each room.

7. Finally, end at the front door. Use the smoke to cleanse the door handles, and then fan the smoke out the door, affirming your intention.

8. Place the dish and burning bundle on your altar. You can allow it to go out naturally or snuff it out like a cigar.

CREATE ENERGETIC WARDS

Once you have cleared your space of unwanted energies, you can create wards that will continue to clear, ground, and protect the energy of your sacred space. One of the easiest ways to create a powerful ward for your home is to use black tourmaline, a powerful protection stone.

TIME: 30 minutes

MATERIALS

Dried rosemary or cedar bundle (for burning)

Fire-safe dish

Feather or wing fan

4 black tourmaline pieces

Lighter or matches

1. It is best to perform this ritual right after a cleansing ceremony. Once you have cleansed the entire space, return to the ground floor, with the rosemary bundle burning in its dish, the feather, and the black tourmaline. Light the rosemary bundle again if it goes out.

2. Intuitively choose one of the corners of the ground floor to begin. You will move in a counterclockwise motion from that corner.

3. Standing in front of the first corner, hold a piece of black tourmaline in the smoke, calling on the allies by name and intention: "Black tourmaline and rosemary for protection and cleansing of this sacred space."

CONTINUED →

4. Place the crystal in the corner and then fan the smoke onto the crystal and then up the corner until you reach the ceiling. Repeat your intention and move counterclockwise to the next corner until all four corners are complete.

5. Once all four crystals have been placed, move into the center of the room with the fire-safe dish in your hands. Spin three times in a counterclockwise motion while repeating your intention.

6. When you wish to cleanse your sacred space again, the first step is to collect the black tourmaline from the corners and place them in the fire-safe dish until the cleansing ceremony is completed. Then, you can re-create this ward using the same crystals.

CRAFT YOUR OWN UNCROSSING OIL

Uncrossing oil is a magical tool to help you break any negative attachments or energies that have been placed upon you by others. This spell oil has origins in African and Caribbean traditions, with roots in Hoodoo and Conjure traditions by enslaved Africans. Uncrossing oil can be used by rubbing the oil all over the body and then showering to rinse it off (and rinse the energy down the drain). It can also be added to ritual bathwater, and after you soak in it, you can allow the water to drain fully and follow up with a rinse in the shower.

TIME: 15 minutes prep, plus 7 days to brew, plus 10 minutes to complete

MATERIALS

2 mason jars

¼ cup dried rosemary

2 tablespoons cloves

2 tablespoons sea salt

10 drops lavender essential oil

Spoon

2 cups olive oil

Fine mesh strainer

Label

Permanent marker

1. In a clean, dry mason jar, combine your herbal allies (rosemary, cloves, salt, and lavender). As you add each ingredient, call it by name and intention: "Rosemary for protection. Cloves for cleansing and luck. Salt for purification and banishment. Lavender for psychic protection and clarity."

2. Next, spoon the olive oil into the jar, covering the herbs in olive oil and stirring the mixture in a counterclockwise motion to banish any negativity. State your intention: "I rid myself of any negative energy and attachments."

CONTINUED →

3. Seal the mason jar and place it in a cool, dark cabinet for at least one week. Check on it daily, repeating your intention each time. You can even give it a little counterclockwise swirl.

4. Once the oil is ready, strain it into the second clean, dry mason jar, repeating your intention.

5. Seal the jar. Label your creation with the title, ingredients, and date of creation.

6. Your oil is now ready to use, or it can be stored for the future.

CLEANSING RITUAL BATH

This ritual bath is a great way to rid yourself of any negative energy you may have taken on. This can be performed any time you feel you need it, especially after a cleansing ceremony or a particularly trying and tense day. The herbal allies in this ritual bath will help purify and protect your energy—your most valuable resource.

TIME: 30 minutes

MATERIALS

Small spoon

2 tablespoons dried rosemary or cedar

2 tablespoons dried lavender

Cloth or organza drawstring sachet

Bathtub

10 to 12 drops essential oils of your choice

2 cups sea salt

1. Using a small spoon, start by adding all of the rosemary or cedar and the lavender to the sachet, calling them by name and intention as you do: "[Rosemary/cedar] for protection. Lavender for peace and serenity." Tie the sachet closed.

2. Next, start to run the bathwater and add the essential oils. Choose and add them intuitively. Place the sachet in the water as well.

3. After the oils and sachet are added, take a moment to breathe over your bath water as it continues to run. State your intention: "I purify and protect my energy." Sometimes I like to "write" my intention in the water with my fingertip.

CONTINUED →

4. Add the sea salt to the water and say, "Sea salt for purification and banishment of negativity."

5. Once the bathtub is full, turn off the water and step into the bath. As you do, repeat your intention.

6. Soak in the tub for an intuitive amount of time, envisioning negativity being washed out and away.

7. Once you feel complete, take the herbal sachet and rub it on your skin, repeating your intention.

8. Staying in the bathtub, drain the water, and envision all negativity flowing down the drain.

9. Finally, rinse off in the shower, sealing this purification ritual.

A CHARM FOR BANISHING BAD LUCK

This charm bag can be carried with you throughout the day or placed under your pillow. These herbal allies combine to both banish bad luck and attract good fortune. This methodology can be used to create an herbal charm bag for any purpose if you simply swap the ingredients to match your intention!

TIME: 20 minutes

MATERIALS

Small dish

½ teaspoon dried peppermint

½ teaspoon Irish moss

½ teaspoon cinnamon

½ teaspoon dried sage

Small spoon

3-inch square cloth

1 small aventurine or tiger's eye piece

2 to 3 inches twine

1. In a small dish, combine the peppermint, Irish moss, cinnamon, and sage. As you add each herb to the dish, call them by name and intention: "Peppermint for good luck. Irish moss for good fortune. Cinnamon for protection against bad luck. Sage to clear negative energy."

2. With a small spoon, stir counterclockwise first, banishing any bad luck from your life. Then, stir clockwise to attract good fortune.

3. Set down the cloth in front of you and place the stone at the center. Both aventurine and tiger's eye support good luck. Tiger's eye lends itself to protection a bit more than green aventurine, so use your intuition here.

CONTINUED →

4. Next, spoon the herbs on top of the stone, trying to keep the herbal mixture at the center of the cloth.

5. Once the herbs have been added, grab the top left and bottom right corners of the cloth and bring them to center. Then grab the remaining two corners and bring them to meet the others in the center.

6. With one hand, pinch all the corners together. With the other hand, twist the cloth right above the stone and herbal mixture, forming a sphere that encloses all your spell ingredients.

7. Use the twine to secure the sphere and keep the ingredients secure. Use as needed.

CHAPTER 7

Support Your Personal Relationships

In this chapter, you will learn ways to support and strengthen the relationships in your life with folk magic. Often, when people think of relationship magic, their mind goes straight to romantic love, but many of these spells, meditations, and rituals can be used for any kind of relationship, whether it's with a friend, a boss, a coworker, a family member, your partner, or a love interest.

When working relationship magic, or interpersonal magic, you want to set a very clear intention that you are not infringing upon the free will of the other person. For example, if you are crafting a sweetening spell for someone named Alex, after you ground into ceremony, you can state aloud, "Alex's free will remains intact." This is an important step for working any magic that influences another person's life without their express permission, and I recommend it for every spell in this chapter. I do not condone working magic against someone else's will. This caveat allows for the magic to be potent only if it is in line with the desires of the other person, which I believe is the only responsible way to work this type of magic.

A REPARATIVE VISUALIZATION

This is a meditation meant to support you in repairing a broken or tense relationship in your life. Although most relationships cannot be fully restored without reconciliation in the physical realm, this visualization is a great way to prepare for an actual conversation, as it helps you anchor into the energy of forgiveness.

TIME: 15 to 20 minutes

MATERIALS

A comfortable place to sit

1. Start with a grounding meditation (page 51).

2. Then focus on your connection to the person you are hoping to reconcile with. Call to mind their essence—their face, the way they move, their mannerisms.

3. Now begin to feel into your connection with them and your feelings toward each other. What is standing in the way of a pure and loving connection? What must be done to repair the relationship? Sometimes it is an apology, and sometimes it is forgiveness. Often, it is both.

4. Once the truth settles in your heart, take a deep breath in and allow the exhale to transport you to where they are in the world. Envision yourself approaching them.

5. Begin to speak aloud. Give voice to what must be forgiven, to your accountability, to your apology, if one is necessary. Witness the way it resonates in the ethereal realm.

6. Open your heart to the frequency of forgiveness. From this space, speak into your love for this person. Why do you want to repair this connection? Why do you want them in your life?

7. Bring both hands over your heart and imagine the way it would feel for this relationship to be fully mended. How would it feel to know all is well? Anchor into that feeling.

8. Allow your eyes to open and carry this feeling with you throughout any next steps you may take in the physical realm.

A LOVER'S ELIXIR

This elixir is meant to deepen and enhance the love between you and another person. It is most potent when shared with your love interest, especially if the two of you are already romantically involved. However, this can also be used as a love-attracting elixir by simply altering your intention during the creation process.

TIME: 10 to 15 minutes to prepare, plus overnight to charge, plus 5 minutes to imbibe

MATERIALS

Medium pot

4 cups water

1 tablespoon dried rose petals

1 tablespoon dried hibiscus

2 tablespoons dried peppermint

Honey or sugar to taste

Dry-erase marker

Storage bottle

Fine mesh strainer

Refrigerator

Washcloth

1. In a medium pot, bring the water to a boil over high heat. Speak your intention over the water.

2. Once the water is boiling, remove the pot from the heat and add the rose, hibiscus, and peppermint, calling them by name and intention: "Rose for divine love. Hibiscus for beauty and passion. Peppermint for happiness and renewal."

3. Let cool for three to five minutes. While you wait, stir in the honey in a clockwise motion. Say, "Honey to sweeten our connection."

4. Using a dry-erase marker, write your intention on the storage bottle. This can be as simple as your two names written together inside of a heart or as complex as you'd like.

5. Once the elixir has cooled substantially, carefully strain the elixir into the storage bottle. As you pour, speak your intention into the liquid, enchanting it.

6. Place the bottle in the refrigerator to charge and cool overnight.

7. The next day, wipe the bottle clean with a washcloth and drink the elixir with your love. If you cannot share the elixir with them, drink it over the course of three days while thinking of them.

HONOR YOUR ANCESTORS

This is a guide to establishing an ancestral altar to deepen your relationship with your loving ancestors. Once the altar is set up, the oats or rice can be left for about a week at a time, but the drink should be replaced every other day, if not daily.

TIME: 10 to 15 minutes

MATERIALS

Altar space

Fire-safe dish

Dried rosemary bundle
(for burning)

2 small shallow bowls

Lighter or matches

Items that remind you of your
ancestors

1 bottle wine or grape juice

2 tablespoons dry oats or rice

1. After a grounding meditation (page 51), shift your focus to calling out to your loving ancestors. Let them know that you are honoring your relationship with them and making offerings to them now.

2. In the center of the altar space, place the fire-safe dish with the rosemary bundle inside. Place one bowl on either side.

3. Light the rosemary bundle and state your intention aloud. You can say something like, "I call upon my loving ancestors now. I make these offerings to honor you and strengthen our relationship."

4. Next, take the items that remind you of your ancestors and intuitively place them on the altar.

5. Pour the wine or grape juice into the bowl on the left as you say, "Loving ancestors, I invite you to celebrate with me; drink with me!"

6. Pour the oats or rice into the bowl on the right as you say, "Loving ancestors, celebrate with me; eat with me!"

7. Pick up the burning rosemary bundle and circle it around yourself, enveloping yourself in rosemary smoke. Place it back in the fire-safe dish.

8. Note what thoughts and feelings come to the surface as you sit at your altar while the rosemary burns. Do you feel a connection growing? How can it be strengthened?

9. Spend time with this altar each day.

A SWEETENING SPELL

Honey jars are a common type of sweetening spell in folk magic. Sweetening spells are meant to improve your connection to another person and can be used for all types of relationships, depending on your intention and the ingredients used.

TIME: 10 to 15 minutes

MATERIALS

Slip of paper
Writing utensil
Empty jar with a lid
2 to 3 tablespoons herbs for your intention
For love interests: rose and cinnamon

For platonic relationships: tulsi and lavender
1 bottle honey or maple syrup
1 pink, green, or white candle
Lighter or matches

1. After a grounding meditation (page 51), set your intention. Speak this intention aloud.

2. On the slip of paper, write the name of the other person and fold the paper toward you. Place it in the jar as you speak your intention aloud.

3. Add the herbs to the jar, calling them by name and intention. If you are calling in a love interest, say, "Rose for love. Cinnamon for passion." If you are hoping to improve a platonic relationship, say, "Tulsi for peace. Lavender for patience."

4. Next, cover the ingredients with honey, stating your intention aloud.

5. Place the lid on the jar.

6. Select your candle. For platonic relationships, use white. For love interests, use green or pink.

7. Carefully light the candle. Allow one or two drops of wax to drip onto the center of the lid of the jar. Place the flat end of the candle into the melted wax and allow it to cool, securing the candle to the lid.

8. Sit with the candle for the entire time that it burns and seals your spell. Spend this time thinking about your connection to the other person.

9. Once the wax has cooled, place your jar somewhere visible in your home.

STRENGTHEN YOUR BOND

This simple spell is meant to strengthen your connection to another person. Your specific intention can vary, but it should be along the lines of deepening your bond.

TIME: 10 to 15 minutes to prep, plus 15 to 20 minutes per day for 7 days

MATERIALS

Carving tool (toothpick, knife, etc.)

1 unenclosed white pillar candle

1 teaspoon olive oil

Mortar and pestle

1 teaspoon dried rose petals

1 teaspoon sugar

Lighter or matches

1. First, set your intention for your connection with this person and simplify it into just one word.

2. Next, pick up your carving tool and carefully carve your name onto the candle, with the first letter of your name closest to the wick end and the other letters continuing down to the base.

3. Turn the candle 45 degrees and carve your one-word intention here in the same manner.

4. Turn the candle 45 degrees and carve the other person's name into the candle.

5. Once more, turn the candle 45 degrees and carve the one-word intention.

6. Next, pour the oil over the candle and use your hands to spread it all over and into the grooves of the carved words. As you do this, repeat your intention and speak your names aloud. Set aside.

7. Using the mortar and pestle, crush the rose petals and incorporate them into the sugar.

8. Sprinkle the mixture all over the candle, pressing it into the grooves of the carving.

9. Finally, burn this candle over the course of 7 days. On each of the first 6 days, light the candle while speaking your intention aloud and sit with the flame for 15 to 20 minutes, focusing on your intention. On the seventh day, allow the candle to completely burn out, sealing the spell.

LOVE-ATTRACTING SUGAR SCRUB

This charming sugar scrub can be used personally to enhance the love in your life, or you can craft two jars and gift one to the person you are wishing to attract.

TIME: 20 to 30 minutes

MATERIALS

2 teaspoons dried rose petals

2 teaspoons dried lavender

Mortar and pestle

Small pot

¼ cup coconut oil

¼ cup jojoba or olive oil

10 to 12 drops essential oils of your choice (optional)

Mixing bowl

4 cups white sugar

4 teaspoons rose water

1 or 2 drops food coloring (optional)

Spoon

1 quart-size mason jar or 2 pint-size mason jars

1. First, decide if you are creating this scrub exclusively for yourself or to share with a specific person. With that in mind, set your intention.

2. Place the rose petals and lavender in a mortar, calling them by name and intention: "Rose to attract love. Lavender for peace and serenity in love." Crush the rose and lavender into a fine powder using the pestle and set aside.

3. In a small pot, melt the coconut oil over low heat. Once it is completely melted, remove it from the heat and add the jojoba or olive oil. You can also add essential oils for fragrance if desired (I recommend geranium or jasmine).

4. In a mixing bowl, combine the sugar, oil mixture, herb powder, and rose water (you can also add food coloring for a slight tint). Stir in a clockwise motion and speak your intention aloud.

5. Use a spoon to scoop the sugar scrub into the mason jar(s), keeping your focus on your intention.

6. Apply the sugar scrub to your body (either with your hand or using a washcloth), gently exfoliating your skin. Envision that as you exfoliate, you are removing any blockages you have around receiving love. Allow the oils to absorb into your skin for a few minutes. Then rinse off the scrub in the shower.

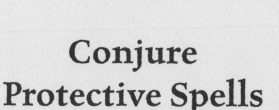

CHAPTER 8

Conjure Protective Spells

T his chapter contains a handful of protective spells, rituals, and meditations to support you as you continue your magical journey. You will learn how to protect your home, yourself, your assets, and more. Remember, protection magic goes hand in hand with cleansing magic, and I always recommend starting with a cleansing ritual before any protective working. Imagine that with protection magic, you are building a fence to keep things out. If you build the fence before clearing the area first, you are just trapping in the things you'd rather keep out! Be mindful of this while working the spells in this chapter.

Intention is very important with protective workings, so as you craft these spells and rituals, keep your intention in your mind, repeating it out loud often. The plants we use in protection magic have so many magical qualities, so when we are calling on them for protection specifically, we want to make that very clear. For example, if you simply use rosemary in a ward, without a specific intention, it is possible to call in ancestral spirits instead. Your intention is *always* key, but with protection magic, it is absolutely crucial.

CRAFT YOUR OWN PROTECTIVE SALTS

Salt is traditionally used for its protective properties, and black salts, rooted in Hoodoo tradition, amplify these qualities tenfold. This spell yields enough protective salts to use in many future workings. These salts can be used on the threshold of your home as a barrier, in charm bags or sachets, or even in a ritual bath for protection.

TIME: 30 minutes

MATERIALS

1 charcoal disc

Cauldron or fire-safe bowl

Lighter or matches

3 tablespoons dried oregano

Spoon

1 cup sea salt

Mixing bowl

Storage jar

1. Close your eyes, lengthen your spine, and center your energy. Ground into the earth (page 51), anchoring into your connection with the land. Intend that you are protected in this working before you begin.

2. Holding the charcoal disc over the cauldron, carefully light one edge of the disc. The disc should begin to sparkle. Place it in the cauldron. Allow it to burn until at least half the disc is gray.

3. Call on the protective nature of oregano as you sprinkle the herb on top of the disc and watch as it begins to burn. Repeat the following intention as the smoke energetically cleanses your space: "I am always protected." Continue until all the oregano has burned.

CONTINUED →

4. Once the oregano has turned to ash, use a spoon to crush the charcoal disc. Stir this mixture counterclockwise to banish negative energy. As you are stirring, repeat your intention.

5. In the mixing bowl, combine the salt and the ash mixture. As you stir counterclockwise, repeat your intention and visualize yourself fully protected in an energetic fortress.

6. Now you can use your salts or pour them into a jar for future use. These can be used any time a protective spell calls for salt.

WARD YOUR HOME WITH MAGICAL FLOOR WASH

Crafting a protective floor wash can be a powerful way to ward your home. This ritual will help you strengthen your physical boundaries. Remember to begin all ward workings with a cleansing ritual like the one in chapter 6 (page 79).

TIME: 35 to 40 minutes

MATERIALS

Bucket

Hot water (enough to fill the bucket)

Cloth or organza drawstring sachet

3 tablespoons dried oregano and/or rosemary

3 tablespoons black salt

Juice of 1 lemon

Large wooden spoon

Mop

1. After a cleansing ritual, fill a bucket with hot water, remembering that water has innate cleansing and purifying properties and can easily be charged with intention. As it fills, speak your intention aloud. It could be something like, "My home is a fortress with strong energetic and physical boundaries. Negativity is unwelcome here."

2. Next, fill the sachet with the oregano and/or rosemary. You could add them straight to the water, but the sachet will keep the herbs from spreading all over the floor as you mop. Call them by name and intention: "[Oregano/rosemary] for protection, physically and spiritually." Add the sachet to the water.

CONTINUED →

3. Now sprinkle the black salt into the water, speaking your intention aloud, remembering that black salt is a powerful ally for banishment and protection.

4. Squeeze the juice of one lemon into the water, calling it by name and intention: "Lemon for cleansing and purification."

5. Use the wooden spoon to stir the floor wash counterclockwise to banish all negativity from your space.

6. Allow the floor wash to brew and cool for approximately 15 minutes.

7. Now you can mop your floors as you usually would, but keep your magical and protective intention in mind, knowing that as you clean your floors, you are putting a powerful protective ward into place.

8. Once mopping is complete, dump the water down the drain. As you do, envision all the negativity that may have been present in your home washing away.

PROTECT YOUR ASSETS

This spell guides you in creating a charm bag to protect your assets and investments. It can be carried with you to important meetings, but it should generally be kept somewhere secure. This is a charm you definitely do not want to misplace!

TIME: 10 to 15 minutes

MATERIALS

Lighter or matches

Dried rosemary or cedar bundle (for burning)

Fire-safe dish

1 small pyrite or citrine piece

1 small black tourmaline piece

1 dollar bill (any denomination)

7 coins (any denomination)

Cloth or organza drawstring sachet

Sprig rosemary or cedar

1. Start with a grounding meditation (page 51), and then bring your focus to your assets. These include your home, your bank account(s), your car, your investments, and the money on its way to you now.

2. Set an intention to protect these assets, something like "My abundant assets are secure and protected."

3. Next, light the rosemary bundle and place it in the fire-safe dish. Both rosemary and cedar are for protection, so call them by name and that intention, speaking it aloud.

4. Begin to cleanse the pyrite or citrine piece, black tourmaline crystal, dollar bill, coins, and sachet by moving them through the smoke. Allow the rosemary bundle to extinguish naturally.

CONTINUED →

5. Put the bill and coins in the sachet, intending that these symbolize your assets as a whole.

6. Add the black tourmaline crystal. Say, "Black tourmaline to protect my many assets."

7. Next, add the pyrite or citrine crystal, calling it by name and intention. Say, "[Pyrite/citrine] to protect my abundant state."

8. Finally, add the sprig of rosemary or cedar. Say, "[Rosemary/cedar] to seal the protection of my assets."

9. Tie the sachet closed to seal the charm.

10. Place the charm bag somewhere safe where it will not be disturbed, like under your bed or between your mattress and box spring.

CREATE A PROTECTIVE AURA MIST

This aura mist is a simple way to incorporate protection magic into your everyday routine. Start your day off by surrounding yourself in a misty cloud of boundary and protection! This mist can help you enhance your psychic and energetic protection, enforcing boundaries against negative energies you may confront throughout your day. This mist can be sprayed on and around your body or in your home as a room spray.

TIME: 10 minutes prep, plus 7 days to brew, plus 10 minutes to complete

MATERIALS

2 or 3 sprigs of sage or rosemary

Mason jar

¼ cup witch hazel

1 small quartz piece

1 (4-ounce) spray bottle

¼ cup spring water

1 teaspoon black salt

Fine mesh strainer

10 to 12 drops essential oils of your choice (optional)

Label

Writing utensil

1. Set an intention for the protective aura mist you are creating. Perhaps, "My mind, body, and spirit are divinely protected."

2. Put your chosen herbal ally into the mason jar, calling it by name and intention: "[Sage/rosemary] to protect my entire being."

3. Next, cover the herb with witch hazel. Witch hazel is purifying, and it will help extract the plant's essence.

CONTINUED →

4. Seal the mason jar and place it in a cabinet for one week. Check on the jar each day and repeat your intention.

5. After a week, gather your materials and center into your intention.

6. Holding the quartz piece in your left palm, speak your intention into the piece. Then place the piece into the spray bottle.

7. Now add the spring water to the bottle. Speak your intention as you add the water.

8. Next, sprinkle the black salt into the bottle, calling on it for protection.

9. Carefully strain the witch hazel into the bottle, filling it completely. Speak your intention aloud as you pour.

10. If desired, add any essential oils calling out to you.

11. Seal the aura mist and shake it up, focusing on your intention.

12. Label the bottle with a title, ingredients list, and the date of creation.

CORD-CUTTING RITUAL

In chapter 7, you learned how to strengthen and repair relationships. However, sometimes we need to completely cut ties with someone. This ritual will help you sever the energetic connection between you and another person or circumstance (like scarcity, or the name of your former workplace).

TIME: 45 to 60 minutes

MATERIALS

Sheet of paper

Metal tray or fire-safe work surface

2 candle holders

Writing utensil

Carving tool (toothpick, knife, etc.)

1 white spell candle

1 black spell candle

1 teaspoon sea salt

6 inches twine

Lighter or matches

Glass of water

1. After a grounding meditation (page 51), start by setting up your work-space. Place the sheet of paper on top of the metal tray and position your candle holders, one on each side of the paper.

2. With the writing utensil, write your intention on the paper: "I, [your name], sever all connection to [their name or the circumstance]."

3. Carefully, carve your name into the white spell candle and place it in the candleholder on the left.

4. Then carve the other person's name into the black candle.

CONTINUED →

5. Use the salt to dress the black candle, calling on its banishing properties and pressing the salt into the grooves of your carving. Then place the candle in the candleholder on the right.

6. Now gently tie the twine around the two candles. Make sure the twine sits about halfway down each candle.

7. Next, state your intention, lighting the candle that represents you as you say your name and the candle that represents them as you say theirs.

8. Sit with your candles as they burn. The twine, especially, is a fire hazard, so keep that glass of water on hand in case of emergency. Notice the way that they burn and how it feels. Once the candles burn out, the spell is complete.

MEDITATION FOR YOUR FUTURE SELF

This meditation is meant to protect you as you journey along your path, ensuring that your future self maintains solid boundaries and securing your current efforts as you manifest your desires and work your magic to improve your life.

TIME: 10 to 15 minutes

MATERIALS

A comfortable place to sit

1. Close your eyes and ground into the earth. As you practiced in the grounding meditation (page 51), feel into that glowing golden root system connecting you to the center of the planet.

2. Draw this grounding and protecting energy up from the center of the earth and into your body with each inhale.

3. With one breath, let energy land at the base of your spine, ensuring your protection. With the next, envision it rising just below your belly button, securing your creative efforts. With another, allow the energy to land just under your rib cage, protecting your personal power. With the next, as it comes into the heart, your energetic field is a fortress. Let the next breath land in your throat, declaring that your words are powerful. Next, breathe into your third eye, the psychic space just above and between your brows, and let your vision of the future be secure. With this last breath, inhale deeply into your crown, opening the gateway into the future.

CONTINUED →

4. Allow your breathing to relax. From here, visualize yourself in the future. What are you doing? How are you feeling? What has manifested for you already?

5. Now visualize that future self surrounded by your spirit team, the loving spirits of the earth and your ancestors, working to protect you on your journey.

6. State aloud, "I am protected here and now and well into my future. My guides protect me as I journey through time."

7. Finally, start to ground back into your body, bringing your focus back to the base of your spine, to that golden root system, and to the physical space you are in. When you're ready, open your eyes.

CHAPTER 9

Craft Doll Babies and Poppets

This particular form of sympathetic magic was very popular in traditional Appalachian folk magic, and it remains a common practice today. Although media portrayals of this type of magic can seem dark or malicious, in reality, poppet magic can be used for curative remedies and to improve the life of the subject in many ways.

In many traditions, different-colored straight pins are used on poppets to represent different energies entering the life of the subject. In pop culture, these pins are depicted as inflicting harm upon the subject. For this reason, I don't include the use of straight pins in my personal practice, and you will not find them used in any of the spells here. Instead, I use dried herbs, oils, and stones to invite in my desired intentions, to err on the side of caution with this type of influential magic.

As when practicing interpersonal or relationship magic, I recommend setting a clear intention not to infringe upon anyone else's free will (page 89). I only condone the use of poppets if you have the full consent of the subject(s). For this reason, many of the spells in this chapter are geared toward creating a poppet for yourself rather than creating one linked to another person. However, they could also be adapted for use with another person with their consent.

THE BASICS OF
CRAFTING POPPETS

Here are some basic guidelines for crafting doll babies or poppets. These instructions will be used and modified for the rest of the spells in this chapter.

TIME: 30 minutes

MATERIALS

Sheet of cardstock paper

Drawing utensil

Scissors

Fabric markers

3 to 4 different colors of embroidery thread

2 (8-inch) squares of fabric for the body

1 (2-inch) square of fabric for the heart

Embroidery thread that matches your fabric for the body

Embroidery needle

Stuffing of your choice (poly pellets, polyester fiber, or even cotton balls)

A method to link the doll to the desired person (nail clippings, hair, photo, etc.)

1. After a grounding meditation (page 51), set your intention for this poppet.

2. Draw the outline of the doll on the sheet of cardstock paper.

3. Cut out the outline and use a fabric marker to trace it onto one of the 8-inch squares of fabric. Stack the 8-inch square with the tracing on top of the other and cut the stack along the lines you just traced.

4. Draw a heart on the 2-inch square of fabric and cut it out.

5. Decide which piece of fabric will be the front of your doll. Using either embroidery thread or fabric markers, create facial features. Sew the heart onto the front of the doll.

6. Thread the needle and begin to sew the front and back pieces together, leaving a gap of about 2 inches so you can stuff the doll.

7. Using your stuffing of choice, begin to fill the doll, ensuring that you get stuffing into the arms and legs. Once you reach the midsection, place the item that links the doll to the person, then continue to fill.

8. Sew the gap closed and finish decorating your doll to your desire.

CRAFT A PROTECTION POPPET

This method guides you in creating a poppet that protects your energy from negativity.

TIME: 30 minutes

MATERIALS

Basic poppet materials
  (page 116)
Fabric marker or permanent
  marker

3 tablespoons black salt
3 small black tourmaline or black
  obsidian pieces
1 teaspoon dried rosemary

1. Ground into the protective energy of the earth (page 51) and set your intention for this poppet. Consider whom you are protecting and what you are protecting them from. Create a short, powerful statement that can be written on the inside of the poppet, such as "I am always protected."

2. After cutting out the fabric pieces, on the inside of both the front and back of the body, write your intention with a fabric marker.

3. As you sew the heart onto the front of the body, leave a small gap and sprinkle a pinch of black salt into the heart. Finish sewing it closed.

4. As you fill your poppet, keep your intention in mind. Once you reach the midsection of the doll, begin to add the items linking the doll to your subject.

5. Add the black tourmaline or obsidian one by one. With the first, state, "My body is protected." With the next, state, "My mind is protected." Finally, with the last, state, "My spirit is protected."

6. Adding the remainder of the black salt, affirm, "Any negative forces in my life are banished from my reality."

7. Adding the rosemary, state, "I call on the power of my loving ancestors to aid in my protection."

8. Finish filling your doll and sew it closed. State your intention aloud, sealing the spell.

9. Keep your doll in a safe place, cleansing it with smoke any time you feel the energy needs to be refreshed.

IMPROVE YOUR LUCK AND PROSPERITY WITH A DOLL BABY

This spell intends to increase the abundance and good fortune in your life.

TIME: 30 minutes

MATERIALS

Basic poppet materials
(page 116)

Fabric marker or permanent
marker

2 small green aventurine or
kambaba jasper pieces

1 small pyrite or citrine piece

1 teaspoon cinnamon

1 teaspoon dried peppermint

1. Center into the abundant and grounding nature of the earth (page 51) as you set your intention for this poppet. Consider whom you are blessing with prosperity and all the ways luck will find this person. Create a short statement based on this intention.

2. Cut out your fabrics, and on the insides of the body pieces, write your short intention.

3. Choose one of the green aventurine or kambaba jasper pieces and sew it into the heart of your poppet, intending that its abundance and love magic will radiate throughout the electromagnetic field of the heart.

4. After filling your doll halfway, begin to add the item(s) that link your doll to the subject.

5. Then add the pyrite or citrine and state aloud, "I am blessed with endless prosperity."

6. Add the second piece of green aventurine or kambaba jasper and affirm, "Luck and opportunity present themselves to me each day."

7. Add the cinnamon and state, "I attract my desires into my life."

8. Finally, adding the peppermint, state, "I am blessed with good fortune."

9. Finish filling the doll. As you do, repeat your intention, then sew it closed.

10. You can place your doll on your altar, especially if you have a section dedicated to finances, luck, or abundance. You can also carry your doll in your purse or pocket if you have a job interview or important meeting.

HEAL YOUR INNER CHILD

Inner child healing is a powerful way to increase your radiance and power. As an adult, giving your inner child agency and love in your current reality allows you to express yourself more easefully as you navigate life.

TIME: 30 minutes

MATERIALS

Basic poppet materials (page 116)

Fabric marker or permanent marker

Mortar and pestle

2 teaspoons dried calendula

1 teaspoon dried rose petals

1 tablespoon sugar

1 small citrine or clear quartz piece

1. Set your intention and create a short, simple statement that can be written on the inside of your poppet.

2. You may wish to create a smaller outline for this poppet, since it is meant to represent the inner child. Cut out your fabric shapes.

3. Using the mortar and pestle, combine the calendula, rose petals, and sugar, calling them by name and intention: "Calendula to support my authentic expression of my inner child. Rose to heal any emotional wounds and increase my self-love. Sugar to sweeten my relationship with my inner child."

4. As you sew the heart onto your poppet, sprinkle a bit of the sugary mixture between the layers of fabric.

5. Write your intention on the inside of your poppet before beginning to sew it closed.

6. Fill your poppet up to the heart, and then begin adding the item(s) that link the doll to your subject. It is especially powerful to use a photo from your childhood.

7. Then add the sugary mixture, repeating the intentions from step 3.

8. Finally, add the citrine or clear quartz, intending that it will aid you as you heal your relationship with your inner child.

9. Finish filling the doll. Sew the doll closed, sealing the spell. State your intention aloud a final time.

10. This doll can be placed on your altar or inside your pillowcase.

USE POPPETS FOR
CURATIVE WORKINGS

This spell provides the basic framework for crafting a poppet to aid in the healing of an ailment. You will need to do a little extra research to find the perfect materials for this curative spell. Check out the Resources section (page 144) for recommendations on some helpful books to aid in the selection of herb and crystal allies.

TIME: 30 minutes

MATERIALS

Basic poppet materials
  (page 116)
Herbs and/or crystals to match
  the curative intention
Extra piece of cardstock paper

Writing utensil
1 small clear quartz piece for
  each part of the body that
  needs healing

1. First, choose your spell ingredients based on the ailment you wish to heal. For example, for an upset stomach, you may choose peppermint, dried ginger, and citrine, as all of these allies are related to a healthy digestive system.

2. On the extra sheet of cardstock paper, list the parts of the body in need of healing and place one clear quartz piece on top of each, intending that those crystals will represent the healing of that body part.

3. Cut out the fabric scraps and write your intention on the inside of the body. Begin to sew the poppet together. If you feel called to include any ingredients in the heart pocket, do so as you craft.

4. As you begin to fill the poppet, place the quartz crystals in the corresponding areas in its body. For example, for healing a broken left foot, add a quartz crystal to the left foot of the poppet.

5. Add the item(s) that link the doll to the subject and any other intentional materials at the heart-center of your poppet, finish filling it, and sew the doll closed.

6. This doll should be kept somewhere safe and left relatively undisturbed during the healing process.

ENHANCE YOUR SELF-LOVE

Crafting this kind of poppet is intended to increase the love you offer to yourself. Oftentimes, increasing our self-love also impacts the amount of love we have to share with the world, increases our magnetism, and helps our dreams anchor into reality.

TIME: 30 minutes

MATERIALS

Basic poppet materials
  (page 116)
Fabric marker or permanent
  marker
Mortar and pestle

2 tablespoons dried rose petals
1 teaspoon jasmine
1 tablespoon sugar
3 small rose quartz pieces
Rose water (optional)

1. Ground into the loving and nurturing energy of the earth (page 51) and set your intention.

2. Write a simplified version of your intention on the inside of your fabric pieces before beginning to decorate them and sew them together.

3. Using the mortar and pestle, combine the rose petals, jasmine, and sugar, calling them by name and intention: "Rose and jasmine to support divine self-love. Sugar to sweeten my self-image and self-love."

4. As you sew the heart onto the poppet, sprinkle in a bit of the sugary mixture and place one of the rose quartz crystals into the heart.

5. Fill the poppet to the heart-center and then add your intentional ingredients. Start with a piece of rose quartz, then half the sugar mixture, then the item(s) that link the doll to the subject, then the remainder of your sugar, and finally, the last piece of rose quartz.

6. Finish filling your poppet and sew it closed.

7. Optional: mist your entire body and the poppet with rose water, intending that your energy is infused with the power of divine self-love. You can use the rose water to enhance the power of this poppet anytime you feel called to do so.

8. This poppet can be kept on your altar, near the mirror you use to get ready every morning, or on your bedside table.

CHAPTER 10

Practice Candle Magic and Fortune-Telling

C andle magic and divination are two of the main types of magic that initiated me in my own witchcraft journey, and I am excited to share some of my favorite spells and fortune-telling methods with you. In this chapter, you will learn how to dress candles for prosperity and open the road to new opportunities, as well as how to peer into the future to understand what lies ahead.

Keep in mind that as you progress on this journey, your psychic senses will continue to activate and elevate. So if at first some of these methodologies seem inaccessible to you, trust that with time, your intuitive abilities will continue to grow. In this way, it may be easiest to start working with an oracle deck or a pendulum before advancing to flame gazing or interpreting candle wax. However, I am always an advocate for exploring more advanced methodologies as a way to open the pathways to deeper intuition and understanding. Trust yourself and allow your intuition to be your guide.

You have already learned some candle magic if you have read this far, but here are some effective ways to include candle magic and fortune telling in your magical practice.

CANDLE COLOR CORRESPONDENCE

Spell candles come in many different colors, and you can enhance your spellwork by choosing a color that aligns with your intention.

White candles signify purification, cleansing, and harmony. White candles can be substituted for any candle color without influencing the energetics of the working.

Black candles are best used for protection, banishment, and shadow work.

Brown candles lend themselves well to grounding and working with nature.

Red candles represent passion, strength, and taking action.

Orange candles can be used in spellwork for increased creativity and vitality and even to ease menstrual cramps.

Yellow candles align with the energy of personal power, manifestation, and positivity.

Green candles are used for nature, love, luck, and money magic.

Blue candles enhance psychic intuition, facilitate clarity, and aid in communication.

Purple candles represent peace, tranquility, and connection to wisdom, especially ancestral wisdom.

Pink candles are used in spells for romantic love, self-love, and harmony.

GAIN CLARITY WITH A PENDULUM

A pendulum is typically a metal or crystal point attached to a chain; it is used to discern "yes"-or-"no" answers as a form of divination.

TIME: 15 to 20 minutes

MATERIALS

1 teaspoon blue lotus petals

Mortar and pestle

Small jar

2 tablespoons olive or jojoba oil

Candle of your choice, to match your intention

Pendulum

Lighter or matches

1. Especially if this is your first use of a pendulum, I recommend creating an anointing oil and dressing a candle before using it. Start by crushing the blue lotus petals into a fine powder using your mortar and pestle.

2. In the small jar, combine the olive oil and blue lotus powder. Say aloud, "Blue lotus for increasing intuition and clarity of vision."

3. Now you can use this anointing oil to dress the candle and anoint the pendulum, repeating that intention aloud as you do.

4. Light the candle, focusing on the intention of this session. What truth do you hope to uncover?

5. Hold the pendulum above the flame, at a safe distance, taking care not to burn your fingers or overheat the pendulum, intending that the flame cleanses the pendulum and imbues it with your intention.

6. Now ask a few questions that you already know the answers to in order to "calibrate" your pendulum, or to understand which direction means "yes" and which means "no." (Example: "Am I in Asheville, North Carolina?" "Do I have brown eyes?") For me, forward-and-backward means yes and side-to-side means no. It can also be a clockwise or counterclockwise motion.

7. Once you get a consistent and correct "yes" and "no," you can begin to ask questions you do not know the answers to.

8. Close the session by blowing out the candle and placing the pendulum on your altar.

AN ORACLE SPREAD FOR DIVINATION

Cartomancy, or using cards to divine the future, has origins in the survival-based trades of the Romani diaspora. This is the tried-and-true spread that I use in my professional oracle readings. It came to me in a dream, and I hope it will be as much of a gift to you as it has been to me! Feel free to refer to your deck's guidebook throughout the reading until you intuitively understand your deck.

TIME: 20 to 30 minutes

MATERIALS

Altar cloth   Oracle or tarot deck

1. Lay the altar cloth in front of you.

2. Start with a grounding meditation (page 51) and begin to focus on opening your third eye. With your eyes closed, pick up your deck and begin to shuffle. Ask that the cards show you the way you're carrying energy now and what that is inviting into your future.

3. Once you feel ready, cut the deck, placing the bottom section on top, and open your eyes.

4. Flip over the first card and place it in the center of the altar cloth. This card represents the core of your energy here in this moment.

5. Next, flip over two cards and place them slightly above the center card, one to the left and one to the right. These two cards represent how you are resonating in your reality and how others may be experiencing your energy.

6. Flip over two more cards and place these below the two you just drew. These two cards represent what is manifesting in your future.

7. Finally, flip over the last two cards. Place one at the very bottom center and one at the very top center. The bottom card represents the deepest work that must be done to manifest your desired future, and the top card represents the highest possible outcome.

8. Take a moment to reflect here, and feel free to shuffle and ask the deck any clarifying questions.

CANDLE MAGIC FOR PROSPERITY

This spell guides you in dressing a candle to generate abundance. This candle should only be burned under close supervision.

TIME: 20 to 30 minutes

MATERIALS

1 teaspoon peppermint

1 teaspoon cinnamon powder

Mortar and pestle

2 tablespoons olive or jojoba oil

Small bowl

Carving tool (toothpick, knife, etc.)

1 unenclosed white or green pillar candle

Small, flat dish to hold the candle

A collection of various coins

4 small green aventurine pieces

2 one-dollar bills

2 cinnamon sticks

2 (3-inch) pieces green string

Lighter or matches

1. After grounding into the abundant energy of the earth and anchoring into your intention (page 51), begin to work on your anointing oil. Combine the peppermint and cinnamon powder using the mortar and pestle, crushing them into a fine powder, and add them to the small bowl, calling them by name and intention: "Cinnamon and peppermint to attract good fortune and divine prosperity." Add the olive or jojoba oil to the bowl and set it aside.

2. Using your carving tool, write either "ABUNDANCE" or "PROSPERITY" into one side of the candle, with the first letter of the word closest to the wick and extending down the length of the candle. On the other side, draw a money symbol.

3. Now dress the candle with the oil you created and place the candle on the flat dish.

4. Surround the candle with the coins and place one green aventurine piece in each of the four directions around the candle and coins.

5. Wrap a dollar bill around one of the cinnamon sticks tightly and fasten it with one of the pieces of green string. Repeat with the other cinnamon stick. Place them on the dish, intending that they generate abundance in your life.

6. Finally, light your candle while stating your intention. Allow it to burn for an intuitive amount of time. When you blow it out, repeat your intention.

CRAFT A ROAD OPENER
SPELL CANDLE

Almost every metaphysical shop will have a version of a road opener seven-day candle, but here is how you can craft your own at home!

TIME: 20 to 30 minutes

MATERIALS

1 teaspoon dried sage or rosemary

1 teaspoon cinnamon powder

Mortar and pestle

2 or 3 drops lemongrass essential oil or 1 teaspoon dried lemongrass

2 or 3 drops cedar essential oil or 1 teaspoon dried cedar

2 or 3 drops peppermint essential oil or 1 teaspoon dried peppermint

Small jar

5 tablespoons olive or jojoba oil

Carving tool (toothpick, knife, etc.)

1 red pillar candle enclosed in glass

Lighter or matches

1. After grounding into the supportive energy of the earth (page 51), place the sage and cinnamon powder into the mortar. If you are using dried lemongrass, cedar, and peppermint, add them now. Use the mortar and pestle to crush the botanicals into a fine powder.

2. Transfer the powder to the small jar. Add the olive or jojoba oil. If you are using essential oils of lemongrass, cedar, and peppermint, add them now. Combine the oils and herbs, calling them by name and intention: "[Olive/jojoba] oil to carry the codes of this spell. Lemongrass to clear the path. Cedar to banish blockages. Peppermint to increase good fortune. [Sage/rosemary] to support and protect me. Cinnamon to activate and inspire."

3. Seal the jar and shake it, focusing on your intention.

4. Using your carving tool, create a few holes in the top of the candle for the oil to fill and rest in. Use your intuition, but create at least four.

5. Now pour the oil over the top of the candle. It is likely you will have oil left over. You can save it for future workings or use it to anoint yourself each time you light the candle.

6. Finally, state your intention aloud and light the candle. Say, "The road to my desires is open, and I overcome any obstacle in my path."

7. Light this candle every day for at least 7 days, or until the candle is completely burned out.

FORTUNE-TELLING
WITH THE FLAME

Flame gazing is a popular form of scrying, which is the practice of looking onto a surface to receive messages or visions.

TIME: 15 to 20 minutes

MATERIALS

2 to 4 drops essential oils to match your intention

1 or 2 teaspoons dried herbs to match your intention

1 tablespoon olive or jojoba oil

Lighter or matches

Candle

Candleholder

1. Ground into the earth's energy (page 51) and begin to bring your focus to opening your third eye.

2. Combine your desired herbs and oils and use them to dress the candle. A simple combination for opening your third eye is the same blend we used in the first ritual in this chapter—dried blue lotus petals and olive oil.

3. Turn out the lights in your space and allow your eyes to adjust for a bit.

4. Close your eyes and begin to focus on your intention. What truth are you seeking?

5. Light the candle and allow your gaze to fall onto the candle's flame. Watch the way it moves and flickers. Soften your gaze.

6. Now begin to ask questions, similar to the way you calibrated the pendulum (page 130). Start with yes-or-no questions that you already know the answers to. Watch the way the flame responds and pay attention to the way that you *feel* when you witness the flame. For me, there is often a lot of flickering and activation when the answer is a "yes." When there is a "no," there is often no response from the flame for me.

7. Once you gain a sense of consistency, you can move on to questions that you do not already know the answers to. Again, pay attention to the way that you feel when the flame responds to your questions. You can start to ask broader questions, like "What will the outcome of [this situation] be?"

8. To close the ritual, blow out the candle. You can reuse the candle for future scrying rituals.

DIVINING WITH CANDLE WAX

This divination ritual can be performed on its own or directly following another spell where a candle was used. If performed on its own, setting your intention or posing your question is a key part of this ritual; however, if you have already dressed a candle or performed a spell with a specific intention in mind, you can use this method to divine the outcome of that spell.

TIME: 15 to 20 minutes

MATERIALS

1 pillar candle of your choice, to match your intention

Lighter or matches
Glass of cold water

1. Anchor into your intention for this divination ritual. What truth are you seeking? What are you trying to understand?

2. If your candle has not already been burning from a previous spell, light it, focusing on your intention, and allow it to burn and create a pool of wax. As it burns, continue to focus on your intention.

3. Once a pool of wax has melted, carefully tip the candle over, pouring the wax into the glass of cold water.

4. Blow out the candle and set it to the side.

5. As the wax hits the water, it will begin to form shapes and harden. Watch this process and notice what feelings arise for you.

6. First, feel into the shapes and their messages while the wax is in the water. What is coming through for you? How can you interpret and glean meaning from these shapes?

7. Next, take the wax pieces out of the water, viewing them from all angles. Continue to sense into their meaning. How do they make you feel?

8. Once you feel complete, you can either bury, flush, or throw out your wax—or, if you feel called to keep it on your altar, you can do that as well.

· A FINAL WORD ·

What a journey so far! I hope this book has been a helpful ally to you as you begin your voyage into Appalachian witchcraft, and that within these pages, you have found reflections of yourself and a deep remembrance of how powerful you truly are. Now, with this foundation laid, I hope that you continue in the exploration of all the magic this world has to offer, knowing that your intuition is your most powerful guide, your wisest resource.

As you craft your magic and hone your wisdom, I hope that you feel the deeply rooted presence of your Appalachian ancestors encouraging you along the way. Remember that this practice is meant to aid you in improving your life and making the world a better place. I hope that, in some way, this book has helped empower you to create the life you have always dreamed of living.

Because of all of those who came before us, we are able to practice magic that makes us feel divine, protected, and radiantly blissful. I hope that the magic contained in these pages has reminded you of your magical birthright and your innate gifts. It has been an honor to pour my heart's magic into this book and walk alongside you as you begin this journey. As you continue along this path, know that I'm holding a vision of you as a powerful Appalachian witch.

So it is.

· RESOURCES ·

The Book of Stones by Robert Simmons and Naisha Ahsian
I consider _The Book of Stones_ the crystal bible. Its index allows you to search by magical or curative intention to find the stones perfect for your spellwork.

Boundaries and Protection by Pixie Lighthorse
This work from Lighthorse is a powerful guide to setting and maintaining boundaries across many areas of life. I highly recommend reading it prior to working protection magic.

Cunningham's Encyclopedia of Magical Herbs by Scott Cunningham
This is an incredible resource for selecting herbal allies for spellwork. There are many guides on the market, but I've found that Cunningham's is the most thorough when it comes to the magical influence of each herb.

The Earth Path by Starhawk
Starhawk is most famous for _The Spiral Dance_, but _The Earth Path_ is an incredible resource providing insights into working in rhythm with the earth.

Maia Toll's Wild Wisdom Collection (_The Illustrated Herbiary, The Illustrated Crystallary, The Illustrated Bestiary, and Wild Wisdom Companion_)
Toll's books and oracle decks are a powerful way to study animal, plant, and crystal spirits. She owns an herbal shop in Asheville, North Carolina.

Mirrors in the Earth by Asia Suler
Another Appalachian practitioner, Suler has many offerings as One Willow Apothecaries, but her newly released book is a powerful look into her journey of self-healing with the earth.

The Modern Witchcraft Guide to the Wheel of the Year by Judy Ann Nock
While there are many books on this topic, I find that Nock's guide to the Wheel of the Year (the Sabbats) is a comprehensive introduction to the different magical holidays.

Native-Land.ca
Native Land is an online resource that helps you understand the Indigenous territories and histories of the land. This can inform your land-based practice and direct you to local land-back movements.

Witchery by Juliet Diaz
Juliet Diaz is a revolutionary voice in the witchcraft community, and her book _Witchery_ is a comprehensive guide to beginning a witchcraft practice.

·REFERENCES·

Editors of Encyclopedia Britannica. Last updated January 22, 2018. "Appalachian Mountains." Encyclopedia Britannica, Inc. Accessed July 29, 2022. britannica .com/place/appalachian-mountains/geology.

Editors of Encyclopedia Brittanica. Last updated May 16, 2017. "Appalachian Orogenic Belt." Encyclopedia Britannica, Inc. Accessed July 29, 2022. britannica .com/place/appalachian-orogenic-belt.

"The Holy Bible: New International Version." Accessed July 29, 2022. web.mit.edu/ jywang/www/cef/Bible/NIV/NIV_Bible/bookindex.html.

Wigington, Patti. Last updated December 28, 2019. "Appalachian Folk Magic and Granny Witchcraft." LearnReligions.com. learnreligions.com/ appalachian-folk-magic-4779929.

· GLOSSARY ·

anointing: Intentionally rubbing oil onto an item, such as a candle, to increase its potency in spellwork

charm: A talisman or an expression imbued with magical intention. Charms can be physical items, or they can be sentences or rhymes that are spoken or sung aloud.

dressing: Similar to anointing, to "dress" an item is to cover it with oils, herbs, and stones that align with the intention of your spellwork.

folk magic: The magical practices of a specific group of people

foraging (or wildcrafting): Sustainably collecting materials from the earth rather than purchasing them from a store

grimoire: A book of spells that typically includes step-by-step instructions, outcomes, and reflections from the practitioner. These can be passed down through a family line.

grounding: Energetically connecting with the earth to create a calm, stable foundation in your internal energetic landscape

herbal allies (or crystal allies): These are herbs or stones that lend themselves to powerful magical intentions in spellwork.

oracle deck: Similar to tarot decks, an oracle deck is a set of cards, each representing a specific meaning or archetype that can be used for divination. Unlike tarot, oracle decks do not follow the organization of the suits, nor the Major and Minor Arcana. Instead, each oracle deck is completely unique.

poppet: A form of sympathetic magic in which a doll is created and symbolically linked to a person to have influence over them.

sabbats: The magical holidays that mark the Wheel of the Year. Learn more about the sabbats in the Resources section (page 144).

scrying: The practice of looking at a surface to receive messages or visions

tarot deck: Similar to oracle decks, tarot decks are sets of cards used in divination. Most tarot decks follow a specific deck structure and have a total of 78 cards, with 22 in the Major Arcana and 56 in the Minor Arcana.

third eye: Thought to be connected to the pineal gland in your brain, the third eye is an energetic center (or chakra) that rules psychic vision, clarity, and insight.

· INDEX ·

Acknowledgments

It would be nearly impossible to thank every single person who has influenced me throughout my magical journey, so instead, I will try to keep this brief.

To all my parents and grandparents, thank you for always believing in me and supporting my dreams—even when they seem out of this world.

To my MaDot, thank you for opening the doorway into the intuitive realm and gifting me with a family who believes psychic activation is possible.

To all my mentors and teachers, thank you for giving me the opportunity to learn from you.

About the Author

Auburn Lily found her home in Appalachia thirteen years ago. She was a dormant mystic, and the magic in the mountains awakened her from a spiritual slumber. Fueled by a curious mind and psychic bloodline, Auburn began her spiritual journey through the lens of mysticism and magic. Introverted by nature, for years she tended to her craft in the shadows. In late 2017, she found herself answering a new and exciting call to share her magic and, most important, inspire others to do the same. She now works in the healing arts, offering online classes and cultivating a community to support others in their magical awakenings. Find out more at auburnlily.com.